ifast

Book One: Forty Days of Spiritual Development

CEPHAS KAFUI

To: Dorrell Dunkley

Blessings.

Doxie Johnson

CREDITS

My express gratitude to Dr. Juliet Appiah (MD) for sponsoring this publication. To Honorable Vivienne E. Gordon-Uruakpa for dedicating her precious time to edit this work. Finally, to Daniel Essuah of Image and Likeness Studio, for the book cover design and other promotional work done for this book.

CONTENTS

PREFACE

A Survey of the Unleashing of God's Power Through Prayer and Fasting in the Early Church to the 1952 Proclamation of the National Day of Prayer

The church was birthed after 120 disciples gathered in the Upper-room in fasting and prayer. Jesus had made it clear that His disciples will have to fast after His ascension. At the Upper-room experience, the disciples, wielded and cultivated through fasting and prayer, the power to change the world.

Paul, the greatest apostle of the New Testament age and the first century church, declared that he fasted often and lived a lifestyle of fasting.

1

History will later testify that the early Christian Church, from the first century to the fifth century, fasted on Wednesdays and Fridays. The church fathers like Jerome, Ignatius, Athanasius, Clement of Rome, Didache, John Chrysostom, Augustine, who took over from the Apostles, practiced fasting. One day a week, twice a week, whole weeks, even whole months were often dedicated to fasting!

Martin Luther, the founder of the Lutheran Church and the initiator of the Protestant Reformation, was criticized because he fasted too much. The renowned church theologian, John Calvin fasted and prayed until most of Geneva turned to God. John Knox, the early father of the Presbyterian Church, fasted and prayed until then infamous bloody Mary, Queen of Scotland said, "I fear the prayers of John Knox more than all the assembled armies of Europe."

John Wesley, the founder of the Methodist Church, when he was a young preacher, fasted twice a week, and kept it as a life-long practice. He records in his diary that at 3 o'clock in the morning, whilst they were fasting and praying, the Holy Spirit fell. His bosom friend, John Fletcher, was known to fast on bread and milk alone on a daily basis for his entire life-time. John Wesley, recorded that, Fletcher, stained the walls of his room with prayer and fasting; for he prayed eight hours a day.

Charles Spurgeon, a Baptist preacher from a century ago, often referred to as the Prince of Preachers, and the greatest preacher since Apostle Paul, practiced long seasons of fasting in his church. Spurgeon who at the time pastored the largest church in England said, "Our seasons of fasting and prayer at the Tabernacle have been high days indeed; never has Heaven's gate stood wider; never have our hearts been nearer the central Glory."

Jonathan Edwards, who was God's instrument in the revival in New England, fasted and prayed. He fasted for 22 hours prior to preaching his famous sermon, "Sinners in the Hands of an Angry God."

What can be said of the greatest revivalist of the 18th century, Charles G. Finney, a lawyer who was used by God mightily? He was a man of prayer, but little is known and said about two men who were in hiding as they fasted and prayed for him. Leonard Ravenhill tells the story of these two men, Daniel Nash and Abel Clary: "I met an old lady who told me a story about Charles Finney that has challenged me over the years. Finney went to Bolton to minister, but before he began, two men knocked on the door of her humble cottage, wanting lodging. The poor woman looked amazed, for she had no extra accommodations. Finally, for about twenty-five cents a week, the two men, none other than Fathers Nash and Clary, rented a dark and damp cellar for the period of the Finney meetings (at least two weeks), and there in that self-chosen cell, those prayer partners battled the forces of darkness."

D. L. Moody, considered the most celebrated evangelist in American Christian history was not unfamiliar with fasting and praying. During the Prayer Revival in America in 1859, Christians fasted during their lunch hours and attended prayer meetings in churches near their places of employment. In two years 1 million people came to Christ!

Richard Riss, who has documented the mid-twentieth century evangelical awakening in America quotes George Hawtin: "The truth of fasting was one great contributing factor to the revival. One year before this we had read Franklin Hall's book, entitled 'Atomic Power With God Through Fasting and Prayer.' We immediately began to practice fasting. Previously we had not understood the possibility of long fasts. The revival would never have been possible without the restoration of this great truth through our good brother Hall."

Hall's book on fasting and prayer was a major influence in the ministries of Oral Roberts, William Branham, A. A. Allen, O. L. Jaggers, David Nunn, Tommy Hicks, W. V. Grant and other healing evangelists who were raised up in the late 1940s and 1950s.

Billy Graham had the largest conversion crusade in England. He reports fasting and praying during his voyage to England before the great work began!

What's more, we cannot forget the impact of fasting and prayer in shaping the history of this great nation, America (U.S.). History can attest that the United States of America, is a nation, just like the Church of Jesus, that was birthed out of consistent fasting and prayer.

When the first colonists arrived on this land, it was known that they'd declare days of fasting against droughts and against native Indian attacks. Edward Winslow's record of the Pilgrims' experiences, reprinted in Alexander Young's Chronicles of the Pilgrims (Boston, 1841), stated: "Drought and the like considerations moved not only every good man privately to enter into examination with his own estate between God and his conscience, and so to humiliation before Him, but also to humble ourselves together before the Lord by Fasting and Prayer."

In 1668, the Virginia colony passed an ordinance stating: *"The 27th of August appointed for a Day of Humiliation, Fasting and Prayer, to implore God's mercy".*

In 1746, the French Admiral d'Anville sailed to New England, commanding the most powerful fleet of the time – 70 ships with 13,000 troops. His aim was to destroy the colonies of Boston, New York, and Georgia. Nevertheless, Massachusetts Governor William Shirley declared a Day of Prayer and Fasting, October 16, 1746, to pray for deliverance. On that day of fasting, a respected pastor from Boston, Rev. Thomas Prince prayed *"Send Thy tempest, Lord, upon the water...scatter the ships of our tormentors!"* The historian Catherine Drinker Bowen related that as he finished praying, the sky darkened, winds shrieked and church bells rang "a wild, uneven sound...though no man was in the steeple." As the prayer ended, a hurricane subsequently sank and scattered the entire French fleet. It was recorded that 4,000 French soldiers fell sick and 2,000 died that day, including Admiral d'Anville. French Vice-Admiral d'Estournelle who had vowed victory to his nation and Queen, was in disbelief, and threw himself on his sword.

Further in the future, the French army joined forces with the Spanish to destabilize the poor structured army of the American colonies. It was then that Benjamin Franklin proposed a General Fast, which was approved by Pennsylvania's President and Council, and published in the Pennsylvania Gazette, December 12, 1747:

"We have...thought fit...to appoint...a Day of Fasting & Prayer, exhorting all, both Ministers & People...to join with one accord in the most humble & fervent supplications that Almighty God would mercifully interpose and still the rage of war among the nations & put a stop to the effusion of Christian blood."

On May 24, 1774, Thomas Jefferson drafted a Resolution for a Day of Fasting, Humiliation and Prayer to be observed as the British blockaded Boston's Harbor. Robert Carter Nicholas, Treasurer, introduced the Resolution in the Virginia House of Burgesses, and, with support of Patrick Henry, Richard Henry Lee and George Mason, it passed unanimously: *"This House, being deeply impressed with apprehension of the great dangers, to be derived to British America, from the hostile invasion of the City of Boston, in our sister Colony of Massachusetts... deem it highly necessary that the said first day of June be set apart, by the members of this House as a Day of Fasting, Humiliation and Prayer, devoutly to implore the Divine interposition, for averting the heavy calamity which threatens destruction to our civil rights...Ordered, therefore that the Members of this House do attend...with the Speaker, and the Mace, to the Church in this City, for the purposes aforesaid; and that the Reverend Mr. Price be appointed to read prayers, and the Reverend Mr. Gwatkin, to preach a sermon."*

George Washington wrote in his diary, June 1, 1774: *"Went to church, fasted all day."*

On April 15, 1775, the Massachusetts colony, under the leadership of John Hancock, having just four days before the Battle of Lexington, declared: *"In circumstances dark as these, it becomes us, as men and Christians, to reflect that, whilst every prudent measure should be taken to ward off the impending judgments...the 11th of May next be set apart as a Day of Public Humiliation, Fasting and Prayer...to confess the sins...to implore the Forgiveness of all our Transgression."*

On April 19, 1775, Connecticut Governor Jonathan Trumbull in a Proclamation of a Day of Fasting and Prayer, intreated that: *"God would graciously pour out His Holy Spirit on us to bring us to a thorough repentance and effectual reformation that our iniquities may not be our ruin; that He would restore, preserve and secure the liberties of this and all the other British American colonies, and make the land a mountain of Holiness, and habitation of righteousness forever."*

On June 12, 1775, The colonies of the America, the Continental Congress, under President John Hancock, declared: *"Congress...considering the present critical, alarming and calamitous state...do earnestly recommend, that Thursday, the 12th of July next, be observed by the inhabitants of all the English Colonies on this*

Continent, as a Day of Public Humiliation, Fasting and Prayer, that we may with united hearts and voices, unfeignedly confess and deplore our many sins and offer up our joint supplications to the All-wise, Omnipotent and merciful Disposer of all Events, humbly beseeching Him to forgive our iniquities...It is recommended to Christians of all denominations to assemble for public worship and to abstain from servile labor and recreations of said day."

On July 5, 1775, the colony of Georgia passed: *"A motion...that this Congress apply to his Excellency the Governor...requesting him to appoint a Day of Fasting and Prayer throughout this Province, on account of the disputes subsisting between America and the Parent State."*

On July 7, 1775, Georgia's Provincial Governor replied: *"Gentlemen: I have taken the...request made by...a Provincial Congress, and must premise, that I cannot consider that meeting as constitutional; but as the request is expressed in such loyal and dutiful terms, and the ends proposed being such as every good man must most ardently wish for, I will certainly appoint a Day of Fasting and Prayer to be observed throughout this Province. Jas. Wright."*

On July 12, 1775, John Adam wrote in a letter to his wife explaining the Continental Congress' decision to declare a Day of Public Humiliation, Fasting and Prayer: *"We have appointed a Continental fast. Millions will be upon their knees at once before their great Creator, imploring His forgiveness and blessing; His smiles on American Council and arms."*

On March 6, 1776, In his Cambridge headquarters, Washington ordered: *"Thursday, the 7th...being set apart...as a Day of Fasting, Prayer and Humiliation, 'to implore the Lord and Giver of all victory to pardon our manifold sins and wickedness, and that it would please Him to bless the Continental army with His divine favor and protection,' all officers and soldiers are strictly enjoined to pay all due reverence and attention on that day to the sacred duties to the Lord of hosts for His mercies already received, and* *for those blessings which our holiness and uprightness of life can alone encourage us to hope through His mercy obtain."*

On March 16, 1776, it is remarkable to note that the Continental Congress passed without dissent a resolution presented by General William Livingston declaring: *"Congress....desirous...to have people of all ranks and degrees duly impressed with a solemn sense of God's superintending providence, and of their duty, devoutly to rely...on his aid and direction...do earnestly recommend Friday, the 17th day of May be observed by the colonies as a Day of Humiliation, Fasting and Prayer; that we may, with united hearts, confess and bewail our manifold sins and transgressions, and, by sincere repentance and amendment of life, appease God's righteous displeasure, and, through the merits and mediation of Jesus Christ, obtain this pardon and forgiveness."*

On May 15, 1776, General George Washington ordered: *"The Continental Congress having ordered Friday the 17th instant to be observed as a Day of Fasting, Humiliation and Prayer, humbly to supplicate the mercy of Almighty God, that it would please Him to pardon all our manifold sins and transgressions, and to prosper the arms of the United Colonies, and finally establish the peace and freedom of America upon a solid and lasting foundation; the General commands all officers and soldiers to pay strict obedience to the orders of the Continental Congress; that, by their unfeigned and pious observance of their religious duties, they may incline the Lord and Giver of victory to prosper our arms."*

On April 12, 1778, General Washington ordered: *"The Honorable Congress having thought proper to recommend to the United States of America to set apart Wednesday, the 22nd inst., to be observed as a day of Fasting, Humiliation and Prayer, that at one time, and with one voice, the righteous dispensations of Providence may be acknowledged, and His goodness and mercy towards our arms supplicated and implored: The General directs that the day shall be most religiously observed in the Army; that no work shall be done thereon, and that the several chaplains do prepare discourses."*

On November 11, 1779, Virginia Governor Thomas Jefferson signed a Proclamation of Prayer, which stated: *"Congress...hath thought proper...to recommend to the several States...a day of publick and solemn Thanksgiving to Almighty God, for his mercies, and of Prayer, for the continuance of his favour...That He would go forth with our hosts and crown our arms with victory; that He would grant to His church, the plentiful effusions of Divine Grace, and pour out His Holy Spirit on all Ministers of the Gospel; that He would bless and prosper the means of education, and spread the light of Christian knowledge through the remotest corners of the earth..."*

On April 6, 1780, at Morristown, General Washington ordered: *"Congress having been pleased by their Proclamation of the 11th of last month to appoint Wednesday the 22nd instant to be set apart and observed as a day of Fasting, Humiliation and Prayer...there should be no labor or recreations on that day."*

These records of US history are no doubt an indication of a nation that has wholly depended on fasting and prayer to breakthrough to the great heights has attained this day. There was no war fought by the United States of America from the years 1782 through 1970, without a declaration of Fasting and Prayer by the Congress and President. During the Civil War, on August 12, 1781, the Union was losing the war, but Abraham Lincoln immediately proclaimed a fast, that changed the tide in their favor: *"I, Abraham Lincoln...do appoint the last Thursday in September next as a Day of Humiliation, Prayer and Fasting for all the people of the nation."*

On March 30, 1863, President Abraham Lincoln in regrettable state after the Civil War, proclaimed a National Day of Fasting and Prayer for the entire nation: *"The awful calamity of civil war...may be but a punishment inflicted upon us for our presumptuous sins to the needful end of our national reformation as a whole people...We have forgotten God...We have vainly imagined, in the deceitfulness of our hearts, that all*

9

these blessings were produced by some superior wisdom and virtue of our own. Intoxicated with unbroken success, we have become...too proud to pray to the God that made us! It behooves us then to humble ourselves before the offended Power, to confess our national sins."

Two years later, when Abraham Lincoln was assassinated, President Johnson declared a National Day of Fasting and Prayer.

In 1918, during World War 1, President Wilson declared a National Day of Fasting for the entire nation: *"I, Woodrow Wilson...proclaim...a Day of Public Humiliation, Prayer and Fasting, and do exhort my fellow-citizens...to pray Almighty God that He may forgive our sins."*

Likewise, during the D-Day of World War 2 in 1944, President Franklin D. Roosevelt called for a National Day of Fasting and Prayer. He believed in the power of God so much in defense of the nation that he stood up to give the prayer for the day: *"Almighty God, our sons, pride of our nation, this day have set upon a mighty endeavor, a struggle to preserve our Republic, our Religion and our Civilization, and to set free a suffering humanity...Help us, Almighty God, to rededicate ourselves in renewed faith in Thee in this hour of great sacrifice."*

In 1945, the United States and the allied nations, won the war. At this great victory, President Truman reinstated the National Day of Fasting and Prayer, and in 1952, that day was officially engraved in the United States history to be observed by all presidents thereafter.

With this great record of fasting, in the history of the greatest nation in the world, can we deny that there's power in fasting? Can we still doubt that God moves through fasting and prayer? If an entire nation bears witness to God's power in fasting, then why wouldn't you and I enter seasons of fasting and prayer until God fulfills His covenant with us. The evidence is clear, fasting is supreme with God Almighty.

The modern-day Christian, the Church today has lost the ancient power of fasting as recorded not just in church history, but in the history of great nations. An understanding of Acts 13:1-13 clearly demonstrates that these three secrets: Worship, Prayer and Fasting, are the wielding agents of Divine power upon the earth. For a while now, churches have captured the secrets of intense corporate prayers, and there is a revival of worship happening throughout our churches today. However, can we change the course of history by adding fasting to prayer and worship? Join me on this forty-day journey of spiritual development, as we once again restore the ancient power of the church, to reclaim our glory, and the immeasurable power of God in our lives.

CHAPTER 1
WHAT IS FASTING?

1

What Is Fasting?

Fasting is a spiritual discipline that is taught in the Bible. Jesus expected His followers to fast, and He said that God rewards fasting. Fasting, according to the Bible, means to voluntarily reduce or eliminate your intake of food for a specific time and purpose.

> *"When you give up eating,*
> *don't put on a sad face like the*
> *hypocrites. They make their*
> *faces look sad to show people*

they are giving up eating. I tell
you the truth, those hypocrites
already have their full reward.
So when you give up eating,
comb your hair and wash your
face. Then people will not
know that you are giving up
eating, but your Father, whom
you cannot see, will see you.
Your Father sees what is done
in secret, and he will reward
you."

Matthew
6:16-18 (NCV)

Why Must You Fast Away From Food?

Man's first temptation was through food. He made a
voluntary decision to disobey and separate himself from
God. It becomes inversely proper that in order for man to
attain his rightful position with God and earn that absolute
intimacy with his maker, he must once again make another
voluntary decision, in this case to deny himself of food.
Fasting is an inevitable practice for any true believer. In
other words, since it was through the desire of food that
the first man Adam was cut off from Jehovah, if you and I
can deny ourselves of food, we can gain access to the
Heavenly realms. Adam and Eve failed God because they
were not able to deny themselves of a particular food.

Today you have an opportunity to seek the face of God by denying yourself food. The question remains, what is more important to you: Food or the Power of God? You decide!

There are many good reasons, and even health benefits, for fasting. However, our 40-Day Spiritual Development is for three primary reasons:

1. Fasting gives you more time for prayer. You can use the time you'd normally spend eating as time in prayer for what God wants to do among us during this Campaign. In the Bible, fasting is always connected with prayer.

   "While they were worshiping the Lord and fasting, the Holy Spirit said, 'Set apart for me Barnabas and Saul for the work to which I have called them.' So after they had fasted and prayed, they placed their hands on them and sent them off." Acts 13:2-3 (NIV)

2. Fasting demonstrates the depth of your desire when praying for something. It shows you that you are serious enough about your prayer request to pay a personal price. God honors deep desire and praying in faith.

   "Declare a holy fast; call a sacred assembly. Summon the elders and all who live in the land to the house of the Lord

your God, and cry out to the Lord."
- Joel 1:14 (NIV)

"Even now," declares the Lord, "return to Me with all your heart, with fasting and weeping and mourning." Joel 2:12 (NASB)

3. Fasting releases God's supernatural power. It is a tool we can use when there is opposition to God's will. Satan would like nothing better than to cause division, discouragement, defeat, depression, and doubt among us. United prayer and fasting has always been used by God to deal a decisive blow to the enemy!

"So we fasted and prayed about these concerns. And he listened."
Ezra 8:23 (Msg)

"God says, "Is not this the kind of fasting I have chosen: to loose the chains of injustice and untie the cords of the yoke, to set the oppressed free and break every yoke?"

Isaiah 58:6 (NIV)

We'll Thrive Only Through Fasting

Man is a little world consisting of heaven and earth. Which is "Flesh = dust / earthly nature" and "Spirit = heavenly nature." It is a true saying that man is first of all a Spirit, who has a Soul and dwells in a house called Flesh. The order is especially crucial in this sense: the Spirit first, then the Soul, then the Flesh. But after man disobeyed God and ate of the tree of knowledge (good and evil), he made a choice to be separated from God. In this sense, the original order changed to: the Flesh, Soul and Spirit. This new order is against God's original design. Man with the help of the Holy Spirit in covenant of the superior blood of Jesus, must make a new decision to avert the failure in Eden. The Flesh must fall, and die in order for the Spirit to gain life and originality. Also, because we are made of the dust of the earth, we are more attached to earthly things and not Godly things. Our Spirit is given from above, and it is more attracted to divine things. So, if we allow the Flesh to reign in us, we will continue to fail in life and be attracted to earthly manners. Likewise, if we fast, we allow our Spirit to gain control and we will be attracted and affected by the divine power of Jehovah and His transcendent glory.

Fifteen Ways You Could Fast

1) All meals for 40 days.
2) 1 meal of juices a day for 40 days.
3) 1 meal a day for 40 days.
4) All meals 3 days a week for entire 40 days.
5) All meals 1 day a week for entire 40 days.
6) Only eat nuts, grains, fruits, and vegetables for 40 days, Daniel's Fast.
7) All juice and drink water only 1 day a week for entire 40 days.
8) All meal fast for half the duration of days
9) Simply greens and water for 40 days.
10) Only drink water for 40 days.
11) Bread and water (or milk) for 40 day duration.
12) Television, Myspace, Video games, Facebook, or other social websites for 31 days (for children).
13) Junk food, desserts, sweets, soft drinks, or chocolate for 40 days (for children).
14) All meals for 7 days, 2 meals a day for 7 days, 1 meal a day for the rest of the Fast.
15) Fasting away from specific foods by revelation for 40 days (I had a revelation to fast away from peppers, meat, diary products, and salt for 9 months).

Choosing The Right Fasting Method For You

There are many types of fasts, and the option you choose depends upon your health, your doctor's recommendation, the desired length of your fast, and your preference:

- A Water Fast – means to abstain from all food and juices
- A Partial Fast – means to eliminate certain foods or specific meals
- A Juice Fast – means to drink only fruit or vegetable juices during meal times

I know the prospect of going without food for an extended period of time may be of concern to some. But there are ways to ensure that your body is getting the nutrients it needs, so you can remain safe and healthy during your fast.

Ten Things You Can Expect:

1) You can expect it to be challenging and difficult. This will take discipline and focus on your part. Disciples are known by their discipline.
2) If you'll stick to your commitment to the LORD you should see a great increase in your faith and your personal spiritual transformation.
3) God may answer your prayer request during these 40 days, but He may not. There is no way for

people to know exactly what God is going to do. We do know that during this time of fasting, we will draw closer to the LORD and that is our responsibility. One way or the other, God will do something during or after 40 days.

4) You will be more sensitive to God's Holy Spirit in your life. Removing the necessities and distractions of life will add a new sense of clarity to the voice of God.

5) You will have an increased fellowship with God and have a greater understanding of what it means to depend upon Him to meet your needs. The biblical word for this is the Supplication of God.

6) You should find yourself praying more direct prayers throughout the day. Your prayer life will astronomically grow.

7) You should expect an increase in spiritual tension and resistance from the Devil. The Bible doesn't speak at all on the physical dangers of fasting. However, on several occasions it mentions the spiritual danger of fasting, specifically the pride and acknowledgement of being a devoted, zealous and admirable disciple.

8) Expect nothing short of a Divine Visitation and escalated Favor for your family, church and friends.

9) You can expect POWER from on-high. You'll be taping into an unlimited divine power reservoir.

10) You'll gain access to the deepest things of God and the supernatural. Your spiritual eyes will open and you'll experience strange but powerful supernatural encounters.

A Message To Families About Prayer And Fasting Together

Your children may hear you speak about your prayer and fasting with much anticipation. They may wonder if this is something that they can do along with their family, and the answer is yes! Explain to your children that fasting will help them grow stronger as a Christian and closer to Jesus. When they take special time out to pray to Jesus and at the same time, take special effort to not enjoy a favorite food /snack item or activity during a certain period of time, they are fasting. As a family, sit down together and talk about for whom or what your children are seeking God and in which way they are going to fast. Then, have your children write down their decisions, just as you will and seal it in a self-addressed envelope with no names on it. We will collect the sealed envelopes during our prescribed services. Explain to your children that there will be times when they will find it hard to fast and may even want to change their minds in the middle of the fast. However, as parents, gently encourage them and help them keep the commitment they made to the Lord and see how He answers their prayers. Following the 40 days of fasting and praying, sit down with them and talk about what the Lord did during this special time. As a family, use the 40th day to break the fast together at a special evening gathering at home.

Moreover, before you begin the 40-day fasting, keep in mind your family's schedule and decide which days of the week you are going to meet together to pray. Be sure to explain in simple words the prayer emphasis for that particular day, so your children can be a part of the prayer time.

Remember that a child's body needs the proper nutrition and activity, as well as rest to keep them healthy and whole. They don't need to fast complete meals or healthy food choices for days at a time or give up the exercise that playtime affords. Children respond best with a set schedule, so be sure to create one in which they will know which days during the 40 days of prayer and fasting that they will be fasting and what exactly they are fasting.

FORMAT: The 40 Days Spiritual Development

WHEN: If fasting alone, you must prayerfully decide, and plan the fasting period as you'd plan a vacation. This will give you the opportunity to spend useful time with God. If fasting with a church, follow the guidelines of your leadership and do not stray from the structure of the corporate fast.

WHY: That we might humble ourselves before our God and ask him for guidance, protection and open doors for us, our children, all our lineage, our community and our nation. You must always have an objective to fast. Read Isaiah 58 for proper guidance on your objective. If fasting with a church, follow the objective of the church fast.

HOW: From 12 twilight to 6:00 p.m., drink only water for

the entire duration of the fast. It is
better to warm your water, and add pure honey, when
possible. You may nourish yourself with prescribed foods
between the hours of 6:00 p.m. to 12:00 twilight. See food
guidelines below. Also restrict your media,
communications, and entertainment activities to necessity.
It is beneficial to use those leisure times for your personal
Bible Study. Listen to Bible on Audio. A good preaching on
the subject of fasting and pursuing God will be great as the
occasion presents itself. Also listen to devotional worships
and praises to stir up your spirit to pray earnestly. The
above time structure is only a recommendation. The time
period for your fasting may change if you're on an absolute
fast. If you're on needed medications, or other intense
activities, you may choose to wisely break the fast earlier at
around 3:00 p.m., or by advice of a doctor or pastor.

FORMAT: In this devotional, we recommend you follow
"The Daniel Fast Principle." Meals are to consist of the
following wholesome foods provided in the guidelines. The
Daniel Fast Principle is chosen as a norm for most fasting,
but you may choose which fast you will do.

READINGS: Isaiah 58: Please read the entire chapter as a
devotional for first one week. We will be focusing the
entire book of Nehemiah for the duration of the fast. Please
read each chapter of Nehemiah per day. Other scriptures
are provided in this guide on a day by day digest.

HELPS: Visit our website for additional resources or email
us. Visit www.prayercell.com or email info@prayercell.com
for further assistance.

BREAKING THE FAST: BETWEEN 6:00 PM TO 12:00AM Twilight

Please be sure to **READ THE LABEL** when purchasing packaged, canned or bottled foods. They should be **sugar-free** and **chemical-free**. Keep this in mind as you review this list of acceptable foods. Fasting is a deliberate choice to avoid certain things, so be deliberate when picking what to eat.

CHOICE OF FOOD: The Daniel Fast Principle

All Fruits (fresh, frozen, dried, juiced, or canned): Including but are not limited to - apples, apricots, bananas, blackberries, blueberries, boysenberries, cantaloupes, cherries, cranberries, figs, grapefruits, grapes, guavas, honeydew melons, kiwis, mangoes, nectarines, papayas, peaches, pears, pineapples, plums, prunes, raisins, raspberries, strawberries, tangelos, tangerines, and watermelons.

All Vegetables (fresh, frozen, dried, juiced, or canned): Including but are not limited to - artichokes, asparagus, beets, broccoli, brussels sprouts, cabbage, carrots, cauliflower, celery, chili peppers, collard greens, corn, cucumbers, eggplant, garlic, ginger root, kale, leeks, lettuce, mushrooms, mustard greens, okra, onions, parsley, potatoes, radishes, rutabagas, scallions, spinach, sprouts, squashes, sweet potatoes, tomatoes, turnips, watercress, yams, zucchini, and veggie burgers (optional) if you are not allergic to soy.

All Whole Grains: Including but not limited to – whole wheat, brown rice, millet, quinoa, oats, barley, grits, whole wheat pasta, whole wheat tortillas, rice cakes, and popcorn.

All Legumes (canned or dried): Including but not limited to - dried beans, pinto beans, split peas, lentils, black-eyed peas, kidney beans, black beans, cannellini beans, and white beans.

All Nuts and Seeds: Including but are not limited to – sunflower seeds, cashews, peanuts, and sesame. Also nut butters including peanut butter.

All Quality Oils: Including but not limited to – Olive, canola, grape seed, peanut, and sesame.

Beverages: Spring water, distilled water, or other pure waters.

Other: Tofu, soy products, vinegar, seasonings, salt, herbs, and spices.

Foods to Avoid on the Fast/Consecration

All meat and animal products including but not limited to – beef, lamb, pork, poultry, and fish.

All dairy products including but not limited to - milk, cheese, cream, butter, and eggs.

All sweeteners including but not limited to – sugar, raw sugar, syrups, molasses, and cane juice.

All refined and processed foods products including but not limited to – artificial flavorings, food additives, chemicals, white rice, white flour, and foods that contain artificial preservatives.

All deep fried foods including but not limited to – potato chips, french fries, corn chips.

All solid fats including but not limited to – shortening, margarine, lard, and foods high in fat.

Beverages including but not limited to – coffee, tea, herbal teas, carbonated beverages, energy drinks, and alcohol.

Acidic fruits, including but not limited to – orange juices, oranges, lemon or lime, grape juices and so forth.

Breaking Fast: Suggested Daily Guide For Juice Fast

If you are beginning a juice fast, there are certain juices you may wish to avoid and certain ones that are especially beneficial. You may find the following daily schedule helpful during your fast.

- **5:00 a.m. - 8:00 a.m.**
  Fruit juices, preferably freshly squeezed or blended, diluted in 50 percent distilled water if the fruit is acid. Orange, apple, pear, grapefruit, papaya, grape, peach or other fruits are good.

- **10:30 a.m. - noon**
  Vegetable juice made from lettuce, celery, and carrots in three equal parts.

- **2:30 p.m. - 4:00 p.m.**
  Herb tea OR simply hot water with a drop of honey. Make sure that it is not black tea or tea with a stimulant.

- **6:00 p.m. - 8:30 p.m.**
  Broth from boiled potatoes, celery, and carrots (no salt).

I suggest that you do not drink diary milk because it is a pure food and therefore a violation of the fast. Any product containing protein or fat, such as milk or soy-based drinks, should be avoided depending on the kind of fast you chose to enter. Be advised products will restart the digestion cycle and you will again feel hunger pangs. Also, for health reasons, stay away from caffeinated beverages such as coffee, tea, or cola. Because caffeine is a stimulant, it has a more powerful effect on your nervous system when you abstain from food. This works both against the physical and spiritual aspects of the fast.

Another key factor in maintaining optimum health during a fast is to limit your physical activity. Exercise only moderately, and rest as much as your schedule will permit (this especially applies to extended fasts). Short naps are helpful as well. Walking a mile or two each day at a moderate pace is acceptable for a person in good health, and on a juice fast. However, no one on a water fast should exercise without the supervision of a fasting specialist.

How To Finish Your Fast In A Healthy Way

Most experts agree that breaking a fast with vegetables, either steamed or raw, is best. Your stomach is smaller at this point, so eat lightly. Stop before you feel full. Stay away from starches like pastas, potatoes, rice, or bread (except for "Melba toast"). Also avoid meats, dairy products, and any fats or oils. Introduce them slowly and in small amounts.

Extended fasts are not the only fasts which need to be ended with caution. Even a 3-day fast requires reasonable precautions. It is wise to start with a little soup - something thin and nourishing such as vegetable broth made from onion, celery, potatoes, and carrots - and fresh fruits such as watermelon and cantaloupe.

In terms of resuming any sort of exercise routine, the advice is the same. Start out slowly, allowing time for your body to re-adjust to its usual regime.

CHAPTER 2

Forty-Day Spiritual Development Guide

2
One Of You

Reading: Isaiah 58 – Read entire chapter to understand God's chosen method of fasting.

Anchor Scripture: Colossians 4:12 [RKJV]

*Epaphras, who is **one of you**, a servant of Christ, salutes you, always laboring fervently for you in prayers, that you may stand perfect and complete in all the will of God.*

In these 40 days of spiritual development, we can carefully observe the character of a man in the New Testament that Apostle Paul gave a special praise to as he writes a letter to the church at Colossae. This man was a prisoner with Paul in one of the Roman prisons. His consistent devotion, and fervent acts of prayer in the prison was greatly admired by Paul. Epaphras, though imprisoned in one of the most notorious dungeons of the Romans, never ceased to pray for his church family at Colossae.

Hence, Paul writes to the church, that though Epaphras is one of you, he is different. Unlike most of you, this man has been restless, praying that God will strengthen his church family and friends.

Can you be an Epaphras for your family, your church, your city or your nation? The world needs an Epaphras amongst us to rise up in these dangerous and perilous times. Can you be an Epaphras in your family, who will wrestle in prayer for the salvation and deliverance of family members? Your church family is breaking apart. Instead of complaining and quitting the church altogether, will you not allow God to use you as an Epaphras to contend for the faith, and the outpouring of the spirit upon your church?

> ➢ You may be one of us, but can you like Epaphras separate yourself from the gossipers, the backbiters, the character assassins, and labor for us fervently in prayer during these 40 days?
> ➢ Can you pray without ceasing prayers that will revive this church, and restore the reputation and integrity of Christianity around the world?

> Are you able to sacrifice with fasting and prayer that your home church will stand perfect and complete in all the will of God?
> Can you struggle with God in prayer, that your life will breakthrough in an exponential spiritual growth?

The Cupbearer Fasted

Fasting Scripture: *As soon as I heard these words I sat down and wept and mourned for days, and I continued fasting and praying before the God of heaven.*
[Nehemiah 1:4]

You may ask yourself, how can I be like Epaphras for my family, my church, my friends, my city or my nation? Or What does it mean to join the Epaphras Campaign?

In this fasting devotional, we will take the life story of a man called Nehemiah who exemplified the Epaphras Campaign and succeeded with remarkable results. Through fasting and prayer, Nehemiah did the impossible with God. You can also do likewise if not better.

Character Study: Nehemiah

➤ He was with the Persian King as cupbearer. In other words, he was a trustworthy and dependable aide to the royal family. He oversaw anything that entered the king's mouth. The best way to kill a king in those days was through poisoning; and a cupbearer had to be loyal, devoted and truthful to be employed, since he was the door to the king's life.

➤ He lived in the Persian capital or the seat of the royal kingdom called Shushan.

➤ He was a layman; not a priest like Ezra, or a prophet like Isaiah.

➤ Israel had been in Persian captivity or bondage for 70 years.

➤ After 70 years were accomplished, Daniel prayed for the divine intervention to activate the release of his people.

➤ Zerubbabel then led the first batch of the freed Israelites to Jerusalem to rebuild the nation.

➤ Ezra led the second batch of the freed Israelites to rebuild the temple at Jerusalem.

➤ After 12 years, Nehemiah took a vacation from the Persian King, as his cupbearer. He asked permission to travel to Jerusalem to rebuild the city. Hanani his brother brought news to him four months earlier that the lifestyle in Jerusalem was very bad.

In this devotion we will observe five things Nehemiah did:

1. I sat down
2. I wept
3. I mourned for days
4. I continued in fasting
5. I prayed before the God of heaven.

CHAPTER 3

WEEK I: I Sat Down

*And it came to pass, when I heard these words, that I sat down ... **before the God of heaven.***
– Nehemiah 1:4 –

3

WEEK ONE: I Sat Down

*As soon as I heard these words I sat
down and wept and mourned for days,
and I continued fasting and praying
before the God of heaven.*
[Nehemiah 1:4]

Hanani, the brother of Nehemiah travels for five months to
visit Nehemiah in the Persian Palace. He tells him about the
state of Jerusalem, and how things aren't going right.

Nehemiah took the message to heart; he was immediately
moved to self-restriction and examination.

- Have you sat to consider your present state or condition?
- When you heard about what is happening in your family what action did you take?
- When you heard that disturbing dream, did you sit down to consider it?
- Looking at the present state of our church, have you sat to consider what can be done?
- Have you sat down in civil protest to the circle of problems and mishaps in your life?

Nehemiah said, the first thing I did when Hanani told me how bad things were in my hometown, was that "I sat down".

- In these 40 days of fasting and prayer, do not move about as you will normally do unless it is crucial. Unless you must go to work or church or an important meeting, restrict your steps during the 40 days and allow God to speak to you.
- Many times we do not hear the voice of God because we do not sit to spend time with Him.
- Throughout the year we have been in haste; moving from work to home and home to work; from one activity to another. We run to church and come home and head on to the next activity on our schedule. We do not sit and meditate on the Word of God, or allow Him to feed us His thoughts for our lives.

➤ This fasting is an opportunity to restrict our steps. To take a deliberate decision to sit home and seek the voice of God.

➤ If anyone will shut-out everyone, and shut-in with God during the duration of the fast; with nothing but God alone and His Word, I guarantee a supernatural move that no eyes has ever seen before.

DAY 1

Prayerfully read the first chapter of the book of Nehemiah and observe his immediate response to the problem.

Make a decision today to sit with God; devote more time to Him or spend more time alone with Him in your personal prayer closet.

Today is the first day of something new. Regardless of where you are in your relationship with God, 40 days of prioritizing the Lord over essential needs in your life, will draw you closer to him and transform whatever needs to change. So today pray that God will help you to envision how you will resemble him more closely at the end of these 40 days.

LOG-ON: Morning Prayers

Begin with thanksgiving and acknowledge the LORD. Confess your sins and receive deliverance and forgiveness. Make amends with people you have hurt or those who have hurt you. Pray for those you despite, those that persecute you and seek your harm. Forgive your offenders and enter the throne room of God with a heart that is pure and blameless.

Enter and make these declarations over your life (pray each point at least 5 minutes; this is will give you a total of at least 60 minutes in morning prayer).

1. Under the covering of the Superior Blood of Jesus Christ, I forgive all those who have offended me (name each person you can remember and forgive them, and ask God's blessings on their lives).

2. Under the covering of the Superior Blood of Jesus Christ, I ask for divine mercy for anyone I have sinned against. (Identify each person, and what you have done wrong and pray for forgiveness) in Jesus name.

3. Under the covering of the Superior Blood of Jesus Christ, I declare I am forgiven of any sins of guilt in my soul and spirit. Pray and forgive yourself.

4. Under the covering of the Superior Blood of Jesus Christ, I confess, believe and declare that Jesus Christ is my LORD, Master, and Savior: I forfeit all ties with my sinful nature and plead the exemption of the Superior Blood against impending judgment ordained for my sins and trespasses.

5. Under the covering of the Superior Blood of Jesus Christ, LORD give me strength in my weakness,

sustain me with your Spirit Divine, and break every yoke and bondage of immorality in my life, in Jesus name.

6. Under the covering of the Superior Blood of Jesus Christ, I escape every arrows of diabolical influence to blindfold me and lead me into sin, the lust of the flesh, and prisoner to lies, gossips, backbiting, and blackmailing. In Jesus name.

7. Under the covering of the Superior Blood of Jesus Christ, I plead for absolute deliverance from any habitual sins I am struggling with.

8. Under the covering of the Superior Blood of Jesus Christ, have mercy upon me, O God, according to thy loving-kindness: according unto the multitude of thy tender mercies blot out my transgressions.

9. Under the covering of the Superior Blood of Jesus Christ, My Father, create in me a clean heart, O God; and renew a right spirit within me.

10. Under the covering of the Superior Blood of Jesus Christ, LORD, restore unto me the joy of thy salvation; and uphold me with thy free spirit.

11. Under the covering of the Superior Blood of Jesus Christ, I receive the unction to function today and to be an overcomer over anything that draws me away from God, in Jesus name.

12. Begin to thank God for strength and His enablement to begin and complete this fast. O LORD I declare you're the author and finisher of my faith. What you have started with me, you shall finish it in Jesus name.

LOG-OFF: Evening Prayers

Acknowledge the LORD with praise and worship. Thank Him and rejoice in His loving-kindness and goodness toward you.

Enter and make these declarations over your life (pray each point at least 5 minutes; this is will give you a total of at least 60 minutes in evening prayer).

1. Under the covering of the Superior Blood of Jesus Christ, Loving Father, I choose to forgive everyone in my life, including myself, because You have forgiven me. Thank You, Lord, for this grace.
2. Under the covering of the Superior Blood of Jesus Christ, I forgive myself for all my sins, faults and failings, especially _____.
3. Under the covering of the Superior Blood of Jesus Christ, I forgive myself for not being perfect, I accept myself and make a decision to stop picking on myself and being my own worst enemy.
4. Under the covering of the Superior Blood of Jesus Christ, I release the things held against myself, free myself from bondage and make peace with myself today, by the power of the Holy Spirit.
5. Under the covering of the Superior Blood of Jesus Christ, I forgive my MOTHER for any negativity and unloving ways she may have extended to me throughout my life, knowingly or unknowingly, especially _____ . For any abuse of any sort I do forgive her today. For any way that she did not provide a deep, full, satisfying mother's blessing, I do forgive her today. I release her from bondage and make peace with her today.

6. Under the covering of the Superior Blood of Jesus Christ, I forgive my FATHER for any negativity and unloving ways he may have extended to me throughout my life, knowingly or unknowingly, especially_____ . For any and all abuses, unkind acts, hurts, and deprivations I do forgive him today. For any way that I did not receive a full, satisfying father's blessing I forgive him today. I release him from bondage and make peace with him today. If you have children, forgive and release them as well.

7. Under the covering of the Superior Blood of Jesus Christ, I forgive anyone I was in an intimate relationship with, for any negativity and unloving ways extended throughout our time together, especially _____ . For all the wounds of our relationship, I do forgive my them today. I release them from bondage and make peace between us today.

8. Under the covering of the Superior Blood of Jesus Christ, I forgive my SISTERS and BROTHERS for any negativity and unloving ways, especially _____ . If you have no brothers or sisters, pray to forgive any members of society who have hurt you, whether at work, or school or in any public square.

9. Under the covering of the Superior Blood of Jesus Christ, I forgive my ANCESTORS for any negative actions that affect my life today and make it harder for me today to live in the freedom of a child of God. I release them from bondage and make peace with them today, in Jesus' name.

10. Under the covering of the Superior Blood of Jesus Christ, I forgive my FRIENDS for any actions of negativity and unloving ways, especially _____ . For any time they abused our relationship or led me astray, I do forgive them. I release them from all bondage and make peace with them today, in the power of the Holy Spirit.

11. Under the covering of the Superior Blood of Jesus Christ, I forgive MINISTERS and all representatives of the church, especially _____ . I release them all, in Jesus' name.

12. Under the covering of the Superior Blood of Jesus Christ, Heavenly Father I now ask for the grace to forgive the ONE PERSON IN LIFE WHO HAS HURT ME THE MOST, _____. The one who is the hardest to forgive, I now choose to forgive, though I may still feel angry and hurt. Lord, is there anyone else I need to forgive? (pause for silent reflection).

DAY 2

Read the second chapter of Nehemiah. Meditate on his interaction with the King and how God favored him because of his heart of intercession for the Kingdom of God. Take note:

> ➤ Nehemiah did not eat. Though he was working for a secular King, he fasted.
> ➤ No job or activity should prevent you from fasting.
> ➤ The cupbearer of the Kingdom, who had the responsibility of tasting before the King ate, managed to declare a long season of fasting.
> ➤ Fasting opened the doors of favor for Nehemiah before the King.
> ➤ The King was willing to give him a vacation.
> ➤ The King was willing to supply him with any provision and resources he required to do the LORD's work.

LOG-ON: Morning Prayers

Oh what joy it is to fall in His presence and worship Him and adore His great name. Lay it all down before Him this morning. Rejoice, remember not the former things and the former ways, but love the LORD with all you are and bless His good name today.

Enter and make these declarations over your life (pray each point at least 5 minutes; this is will give you a total of at least 60 minutes in morning prayer).

1. Under the covering of the Superior Blood of Jesus Christ, Plant my heart, O Lord in Your ways and create a deep hunger for you in my heart, in the name of Jesus.

2. Under the covering of the Superior Blood of Jesus Christ, Holy Ghost, show me where I have fallen and make me to do the first works, in the name of Jesus.

3. Under the covering of the Superior Blood of Jesus Christ, Jesus, remove not my candlestick from Your presence, in the name of Jesus.

4. Under the covering of the Superior Blood of Jesus Christ, Every power disgracing me before God, BE DISGRACED, in the name of Jesus.

5. Under the covering of the Superior Blood of Jesus Christ, O Lord, let no one defile me anymore, in the name of Jesus.

6. Lord God Almighty, visit me afresh and let Your light shine upon me once again, in the name of Jesus.

7. Under the covering of the Superior Blood of Jesus Christ, Holy Ghost, quicken me and bring me alive, in the name of Jesus.

8. Under the covering of the Superior Blood of Jesus Christ, I shall walk in the light of the Lord, in the name of Jesus.

9. Under the covering of the Superior Blood of Jesus Christ, Plant in me, O Lord, the tree of life for my healing and the healing of the nations, in the name of Jesus.

10. Under the covering of the Superior Blood of Jesus Christ, O Lord, subdue in me, the love of sin, in the name of Jesus.

11. Under the covering of the Superior Blood of Jesus Christ, O Lord, renovate my life for Your use, in the name of Jesus.

12. Under the covering of the Superior Blood of Jesus Christ, O Lord, break pride to pieces in my life and scatter it to the winds, and destroy in me every proud thought in the name of Jesus.

LOG-OFF: Evening Prayers

Enter and make these declarations over your life (pray each point at least 5 minutes; this is will give you a total of at least 60 minutes in evening prayer).

1. Under the covering of the Superior Blood of Jesus Christ, Empower me to live as You would have me do, in the name of Jesus.
2. Under the covering of the Superior Blood of Jesus Christ, Empower me, O Lord, to walk in love and meekness, in the name of Jesus.
3. Under the covering of the Superior Blood of Jesus Christ, O Lord, let me not be at my own disposal, in the name of Jesus.
4. Under the covering of the Superior Blood of Jesus Christ, My name will not be a reproach to the kingdom of God, in the name of Jesus.
5. Under the covering of the Superior Blood of Jesus Christ, Father, come as mighty power and expel every rebellious lust in me, in the name of Jesus.
6. Under the covering of the Superior Blood of Jesus Christ, Father, come as mighty power and reign supreme in my life, in the name of Jesus.
7. Under the covering of the Superior Blood of Jesus Christ, Father, come as a Teacher and lead me into all truth, in the name of Jesus.
8. Under the covering of the Superior Blood of Jesus Christ, Father, come as a Teacher and fill me with understanding, in the name of Jesus.
9. Under the covering of the Superior Blood of Jesus Christ, Father, come as love and make me adore You more, in the name of Jesus.

10. Under the covering of the Superior Blood of Jesus Christ, Father, come as joy and overshadow my heart, in the name of Jesus.
11. Under the covering of the Superior Blood of Jesus Christ, Father, come as light and illuminate the scriptures to me, in the name of Jesus.
12. Under the covering of the Superior Blood of Jesus Christ, Father, come as fire and purify my heart, in the name of Jesus.

DAY 3

Meditate today on the third chapter of Nehemiah. Notice carefully how everyone was willing to participate in the building of the LORD's work.

➢ Take note of their willingness to repair the walls and do their part to secure the Kingdom.
➢ Are you also willing to do your part to build and serve in your local church?
➢ Will you say this day that LORD, I am willing, use me to build your church in anyway possible?
➢ Did you notice the verse 5, that some noble men refused to do the work?
➢ They refused to help build the Kingdom. The Bible said they refused to put their neck or shoulders to the work?
➢ They were uninterested in building God's Kingdom.
➢ May God use you to build and repair every breach in your local church and to lift up the foundation of His ministry. Likewise, may you be used in your family and bloodline to repair foundations and set a standard.

LOG-ON: Morning Prayers

Enter and make these declarations over your life (pray each point at least 5 minutes; this is will give you a total of at least 60 minutes in morning prayer).

1. Under the covering of the Superior Blood of Jesus Christ, O Lord make me the kind of vessel you want me to be in the name of Jesus.
2. Under the covering of the Superior Blood of Jesus Christ, O Lord break me, remold me and use me in the name of Jesus.
3. Under the covering of the Superior Blood of Jesus Christ, O Lord, change my heart and make it new every day in the name of Jesus.
4. Under the covering of the Superior Blood of Jesus Christ, Anything in my life that will disqualify me in the service of God, be uprooted and be cast away in the name of Jesus.
5. Under the covering of the Superior Blood of Jesus Christ, Lord Jesus, walk in every area of my life in the name of Jesus.
6. Under the covering of the Superior Blood of Jesus Christ, the grace to serve God without murmuring, come upon me in the name of Jesus.
7. Under the covering of the Superior Blood of Jesus Christ, the grace to serve God without seeking recognition of men, come upon my life, in the name of Jesus.
8. Under the covering of the Superior Blood of Jesus Christ, the grace to hear and obey Jesus, come upon my life, in the name of Jesus.

9. Under the covering of the Superior Blood of Jesus Christ, the grace to carry my cross and follow Jesus everyday, come upon my life in the name of Jesus.

10. Under the covering of the Superior Blood of Jesus Christ, the grace to die to self and walk in the Spirit, come upon my life in the name of Jesus.

11. Under the covering of the Superior Blood of Jesus Christ, any cataract in my spiritual eyes blocking me from seeing Jesus, be flushed out by the blood of Jesus, in the name of Jesus.

12. Under the covering of the Superior Blood of Jesus Christ, thou demon of confusion assigned to mislead me, be arrested by the fire of God.

LOG-OFF: Evening Prayers

Enter and make these declarations over your life (pray each point at least 5 minutes; this is will give you a total of at least 60 minutes in evening prayer).

1. Under the covering of the Superior Blood of Jesus Christ, O Lord, give me grace to be transformed into Thy likeness, in the name of Jesus.

2. Under the covering of the Superior Blood of Jesus Christ, O Lord, give me grace to be consecrated wholly to You, in the name of Jesus.

3. Under the covering of the Superior Blood of Jesus Christ, O Lord, give me grace to live entirely to Thy glory, in the name of Jesus.

4. Under the covering of the Superior Blood of Jesus Christ, O Lord, deliver me, from attachments to unclean things, in the name of Jesus.

5. Under the covering of the Superior Blood of Jesus Christ, O Lord, deliver me, from attachments to the wrong associations, in the name of Jesus.

6. Under the covering of the Superior Blood of Jesus Christ, O Lord, deliver me, from attachments to evil passions, in the name of Jesus.

7. Under the covering of the Superior Blood of Jesus Christ, O God, arise and open to me the springs of divine knowledge, in the name of Jesus.

8. Under the covering of the Superior Blood of Jesus Christ, While I live, O Lord, let my life be exemplary, in the name of Jesus.

9. Under the covering of the Superior Blood of Jesus Christ, O Lord, fight for me and let my foes flee, in the name of Jesus.

10. Under the covering of the Superior Blood of Jesus Christ, O Lord, uphold me, and I cannot fall, in the name of Jesus.

11. Under the covering of the Superior Blood of Jesus Christ, Stand by me, Lord, and satan will depart, in the name of Jesus.

12. Teach me, O Lord, to look to Jesus on His cross, in the name of Jesus.

DAY 4

Meditate today on the Nehemiah 4 the entire chapter. Take note of the following as you read:

➤ There's always opposition when God begins to do something great in our lives and in our church. Throughout this fast, you might face a lot of opposition; perhaps at your work place, or with your friends or even with family members. This is a strategy of the enemy to cause you to break from your desire to have a better relationship with God. Take heed, and be beware.

➤ As we have declared this fast, the enemy will attempt to thwart our efforts and destroy what God has started amongst us.

➤ But he shall not prevail. He will attempt to make a mockery of our spiritual development, and make our hands weak in doing good for God.

➤ The enemy has a design to frustrate our efforts to develop spiritually, and our success as God's people.

➤ But we can take a hint from how Nehemiah dealt with this same problem. He said, *"Nevertheless, we made our prayer unto our God, and set a watch against them day and night, because of them."* (Neh. 4:9).

➤ Can you also keep watch day and night?
➤ Can you make a commitment to pray fervently for a better relationship with God?
➤ Can you pray for your local church?
➤ Can you pray for your family members and friends?
➤ Set a prayer watch day and night against the manipulations, the schemes and the stratagem of the enemy. You shall prevail in Jesus name.
➤ Prayer did not fail Nehemiah and it will not fail us.

LOG-ON: Morning Prayers

Enter and make these declarations over your life (pray each point at least 5 minutes; this is will give you a total of at least 60 minutes in morning prayer).

1. Under the covering of the Superior Blood of Jesus Christ, I loose confusion against every satanic and demonic conspiracy against my life, my family, my friends and my local church, in Jesus name.
2. Under the covering of the Superior Blood of Jesus Christ, Let the secret counsel of the wicked be turned into foolishness in Jesus name.
3. Under the covering of the Superior Blood of Jesus Christ, Let GOD arise, and let those gathered against my life, my family, and my local church be scattered.
4. Under the covering of the Superior Blood of Jesus Christ, No weapon that is formed against my life, my family, my friends, and local church shall prosper. The gates of hell shall not prevail against us in Jesus name.
5. Under the covering of the Superior Blood of Jesus Christ, I stand as a child of Almighty God to overturn every strategy of hell against my local church and any member, in Jesus name.
6. Under the covering of the Superior Blood of Jesus Christ, Every strategy of hell operating against my life, my family, my friends and local church, is exposed and brought to light, in Jesus name.
7. Under the covering of the Superior Blood of Jesus Christ, I receive the plans of God for my life, my

family, my friends and my local church, thoughts of peace and not evil to bring us to an expected end.

8. Under the covering of the Superior Blood of Jesus Christ, I declare that we, myself, my family, my friends and local church are delivered from every satanic trap and plot in Jesus name.

9. Under the covering of the Superior Blood of Jesus Christ, Let those who devise the hurt and destruction of my life, my family, my friends and my local church be turned back and brought to confusion.

10. Under the covering of the Superior Blood of Jesus Christ, Let the nets they have hidden catch themselves, and into that very destruction let them fall.

11. Under the covering of the Superior Blood of Jesus Christ, I bind and rebuke every spirit of Sanballat and Tobiah operating against the progress of my life, my family, my friends and local church in the name of Jesus. - Nehemiah 4:1-23.

12. Under the covering of the Superior Blood of Jesus Christ, O LORD, Hide my life, my family, my friends, and my local church from the secret counsel of the wicked. – Psalm 64:2.

LOG-OFF: Evening Prayers

Enter and make these declarations over your life (pray each point at least 5 minutes; this is will give you a total of at least 60 minutes in evening prayer).

1. Under the covering of the Superior Blood of Jesus Christ, I break and divide every demonic confederacy against my life, my family, and my local church in Jesus name.
2. Under the covering of the Superior Blood of Jesus Christ, I loose confusion into every demonic confederacy directed against my life, family, and my local church in the name of Jesus.
3. Under the covering of the Superior Blood of Jesus Christ, O LORD, Arise, divide and scatter them that are joined together against my life, my family, my friends and my local church.
4. Under the covering of the Superior Blood of Jesus Christ, I bind and rebuke all demonic reinforcements sent by satan to attack my life, my family, my friends and my local church.
5. Under the covering of the Superior Blood of Jesus Christ, O LORD, Make the ruling spirits of these confederacies be like Oreb, Zeeb, Zebah, and Zalmunna. (Psalm 83:5-11).
6. Under the covering of the Superior Blood of Jesus Christ, Oh my God, for those who have falsely advertised my life, my family, and local church with a mission to tarnish it, make them like the wheel, as the stubble before the wind. (Psalm 83:13).
7. Under the covering of the Superior Blood of Jesus Christ, O LORD, those that trouble my life, my

family and local church to destroy us, persecute them with thy tempest, and make them afraid with thy storm. (Psalm 83:15).

8. Under the covering of the Superior Blood of Jesus Christ, O Father, for those that are on a counter mission against my life, my family and my local church, Let them be confounded and troubled forever. Let them be put to shame and perish. (Psalm 83:17).

9. Under the covering of the Superior Blood of Jesus Christ, Any evil and witchcraft confederacy against my life, my family, my friends and my local church, I loose confusion against you, and LORD, let them attack each other in the name of Jesus. (2 Chron. 20:23)

10. Under the covering of the Superior Blood of Jesus Christ, O LORD, strengthen me to overcome every force of opposition against my spiritual growth and desire to serve you.

11. Under the covering of the Superior Blood of Jesus Christ, Holy Spirit, take charge of my life, rule my body, my soul and my spirit. I surrender to the arm of your power in Jesus name.

12. Under the covering of the Superior Blood of Jesus Christ, I declare, the LORD is my portion, my constant help in time of trouble, I shall not be moved, and I shall not fear.

DAY 5

Read the entire chapter of Nehemiah 5, and meditate on how the people of God were attacked by the enemy in their season of commitment to God.

- ➢ Note carefully that all of a sudden there was civil war among the people of God.
- ➢ They started fighting each other and there was a strong division among them because the enemy had attacked their finances and resources.
- ➢ In times like this when we declare a season of fasting and prayer, the devil always finds a way to dig out problems that will cause division and diversion.
- ➢ But do not be moved by what the evil whirlwind will blow your direction this month.
- ➢ Don't allow the enemy to make you his ambassador of evil devices and schemes.
- ➢ Be in fervent prayer. If you hear any divisive rumors from any circles, even from trustworthy sources, pray to avert that satanic distraction.

➤ Give no room for the enemy to function in your life and to destroy your blessing in this month. We will not fail God this month.

➤ Any wicked advertisement and falsified documentation of the enemy to undermine the power of God in my life, my family, and my local church will fail, for the LORD has not sanctioned it.

LOG-ON: Morning Prayers

Enter and make these declarations over your life (pray each point at least 5 minutes; this is will give you a total of at least 60minutes in morning prayer).

1. Under the covering of the Superior Blood of Jesus Christ, My Father, Let the spirit of the Assyrian be broken in my life, my family, and my local church in Jesus name. *(Isaiah 14:25).*

2. Under the covering of the Superior Blood of Jesus Christ, O LORD, Break in pieces the gates of brass, and cut the bars of iron against my life, my family, and local church in Jesus name. (Isa. 45:2).

3. Under the covering of the Superior Blood of Jesus Christ, I break every yoke from off my neck, my family and my local church; and I burst all the bonds in the name of Jesus. (Jeremiah 30:80).

4. Under the covering of the Superior Blood of Jesus Christ, LORD, deal with the agents and spirits of division in my life, my family, and my local church; break them with the rod of iron, and dash them in pieces like a potter's vessel. (Ps. 2:9).

5. Under the covering of the Superior Blood of Jesus Christ, My Father, Break the arm of the wicked, that their evil schemes and devices will not triumph against me this year. (Ps. 10:15).

6. Under the covering of the Superior Blood of Jesus Christ, Break their teeth, O God, in their mouths, that they'll not be able to bite. Break the teeth of the young lions. (Ps. 58:6).

7. Under the covering of the Superior Blood of Jesus Christ, In my life, my family and my local church, Let the oppressor be broken in pieces. (Ps. 72:4).

8. Under the covering of the Superior Blood of Jesus Christ, In my life, my family and my local church, Let the arms of the wicked be broken. (Ps. 37:17).

9. Under the covering of the Superior Blood of Jesus Christ, in my life, my family, and my local church, Let the horns of the wicked be broken. (Dan. 8:8).

10. Under the covering of the Superior Blood of Jesus Christ, in my life, my family and my local church, Let the kingdom of darkness be broken. (Dan. 11:4).

11. Under the covering of the Superior Blood of Jesus Christ, in my life, my family and my local church, Let the foundations of the wicked be broken. (Ezekiel 30:4).

12. Under the covering of the Superior Blood of Jesus Christ, in my life, my family and local church, Let the kingdoms of Babylon be broken. (Jeremiah 51:58).

LOG-OFF: Evening Prayers

Enter and make these declarations over your life (pray each point at least 5 minutes; this is will give you a total of at least 60 minutes in evening prayer).

Sign off your prayer tonight with a personal prayer for your own Christian growth and spiritual awakening.

1. Under the covering of the Superior Blood of Jesus Christ, Help me, O Lord, to walk as Jesus walked, in the name of Jesus.
2. Under the covering of the Superior Blood of Jesus Christ, Subdue my spirit, O Lord, in Your arms of love, in the name of Jesus.
3. Under the covering of the Superior Blood of Jesus Christ, Deliver me, O Lord, from worldly dispositions, in the name of Jesus.
4. Under the covering of the Superior Blood of Jesus Christ, Deliver me, O Lord, from the spirit of slumber, in the name of Jesus.
5. Under the covering of the Superior Blood of Jesus Christ, Stay my mind on You, O Lord, and turn my trials to blessings, in the name of Jesus.
6. Under the covering of the Superior Blood of Jesus Christ, Lord, let my obedience to Your will be natural and delightful, in the name of Jesus.
7. Under the covering of the Superior Blood of Jesus Christ, Give me, O Lord, complete deadness to the world, in the name of Jesus.
8. Under the covering of the Superior Blood of Jesus Christ, Let my character and conduct preach the gospel, in the name of Jesus.

9. Under the covering of the Superior Blood of Jesus Christ, Let my character and conduct compel people to ask the way to the Master, in the name of Jesus.
10. Under the covering of the Superior Blood of Jesus Christ, Any power assigned to injure the prosperity of my soul, die, in the name of Jesus.
11. Under the covering of the Superior Blood of Jesus Christ, Lord, give me a heart framed to Your will, in the name of Jesus.
12. Under the covering of the Superior Blood of Jesus Christ, strengthen me to give You no rest, in the name of Jesus.

DAY 6

Read and meditate on the entire chapter of Nehemiah 6.

➤ Once again, see how Sanballat and Tobiah came back to interrupt the work.

➤ Once the enemy realizes that we are doing well and progressing by grace despite his wicked designs and efforts, he will increase his momentum of destruction against us.

➤ The devil works through people as he did through Sanballat and Tobiah to stop the work that Nehemiah and the people were doing for the Kingdom of God.

➤ May we also keep an eye on these Sanballat and Tobiah who will come amongst us only to divert our effort, divide us, sing songs of bitterness, conceive and give birth to lies, and evil designs.

LOG-ON: Morning Prayers

Take this opportunity not only to pray for yourself, but also your local church. Anyone that prays for the church, will be defended by God. The LORD will take care of your needs as you pray for His church. Enter and make these declarations over your life and church (pray each point at least 5 minutes; this is will give you a total of at least 60 minutes in morning prayer).

1. Under the covering of the Superior Blood of Jesus Christ, Satan, the LORD Jesus rebuked and defeated you; He made a show of you openly. (Zech. 3:2; Col. 2:15).
2. Under the covering of the Superior Blood of Jesus Christ, Get thee hence satan, for it is written. (Matt. 4:10).
3. Under the covering of the Superior Blood of Jesus Christ, Get thee behind me satan, for it is written. (Luke 4:8).
4. Under the covering of the Superior Blood of Jesus Christ, I declare, Jesus beheld satan as lightning fall from heaven. He then gave me authority to tread on serpents and scorpions and over all the power of satan. I exercise this authority daily, in the name of Jesus. (Luke 10:18, 19).
5. Under the covering of the Superior Blood of Jesus Christ, I release myself, and the operations of my local church from every bond of satan, in the name of Jesus. (Luke 13:16).
6. Under the covering of the Superior Blood of Jesus Christ, LORD, I bind, rebuke and bruise all

hindering spirits of satan operating in my local church, in the name of Jesus. (Rom. 16:20; I Thess. 2:18).

7. Under the covering of the Superior Blood of Jesus Christ, I renounce and disannul all unGodly anger, and I give no place to the devil to operate in my local church and amongst its members, in the name of Jesus (Eph. 4:27).

8. Under the covering of the Superior Blood of Jesus Christ, As a member of my local church, I overcome any sifting that satan would try to bring into my life and I am delivered from the power of satan unto God, in the name of Jesus. (Luke 22:31; Acts 26:18).

9. Under the covering of the Superior Blood of Jesus Christ, In the name of Jesus, I bind the thief from stealing, killing or destroying my life, family, ministry and local church.

10. Under the covering of the Superior Blood of Jesus Christ, In the name of Jesus, LORD, I remove every synagogue of satan and satan's seat working against my local church (call your church name). (Rev. 2:13; 3:9).

11. Under the covering of the Superior Blood of Jesus Christ, I bind and disannul all wrath of the devil directed against my local church and its members, in the name of Jesus. (Rev. 12:12).

12. Under the covering of the Superior Blood of Jesus Christ, As a member of my local church (call your church name), I am sober and vigilant against my adversary, the devil and all his hosts, because he is a defeated foe, in the name of Jesus. (I Peter 5:8).

LOG-OFF: Evening Prayers

Before your sign-off your fasting tonight. Make another bold statement and declare with much prayer that the spirit of Sanballat and Tobiah shall be disgraced in Jesus name. Let God use you to create, and not to destroy; to build and not to pull down.

Take this opportunity not only to pray for yourself, but also your local church. Anyone that prays for the church, will be defended by God. The LORD will take care of your needs as you pray for His church. Enter and make these declarations over your life and church (pray each point at least 5 minutes; this is will give you a total of at least 60 minutes in evening prayer).

1. Under the covering of the Superior Blood of Jesus Christ, I quench every fiery dart the enemy sends against my local church and its members, with the shield of the faith. (Eph. 6:16).
2. Under the covering of the Superior Blood of Jesus, I quench every fiery dart of jealousy, envy, anger, bitterness, and rage sent against my life, family, ministry and my local church, in the name of Jesus.
3. Under the covering of the Superior Blood of Jesus, I quench every firebrand sent against my life, family, ministry and my local church by the enemy, in the name of Jesus. (Isa.7:4).
4. Under the covering of the Superior Blood of Jesus, I bind and disannul all spirits of jealousy directed against my life, family ministry and my local church in the name of Jesus.

5. Under the covering of the Superior Blood of Jesus, I quench every fire the enemy would throw into my local church in the name of Jesus. (Ps. 74:7).

6. Under the covering of the Superior Blood of Jesus, I bind and cast out every fiery serpent sent against my life, family ministry and my local church in the name of Jesus. (Isa. 30:6).

7. Under the covering of the Superior Blood of Jesus, I quench every burning lamp that comes from leviathan's mouth with the Fire of God. (Job 41:19).

8. Under the covering of the Superior Blood of Jesus, As a member of my local church, I am not burned by the fire of the enemy, in the name of Jesus. (Isa. 43:2).

9. Under the covering of the Superior Blood of Jesus, As a member of my local church, I overcome every fiery trial sent against my life, family, ministry and church by the enemy in the name of Jesus. (1 Pet. 1:7).

10. Under the covering of the Superior Blood of Jesus, I declare as a member of my local church, the enemy is not able to burn up my harvest, in the name of Jesus. (2 Sam. 14:30).

11. Under the covering of the Superior Blood of Jesus, I quench every fire of wickedness sent against my life, family, ministry and my local church in the name of Jesus. (Isa. 9:18).

12. Under the covering of the Superior Blood of Jesus, I quench and disannul all unGodly words spoken against me, my family, ministry and my local church in the name of Jesus. (Proverbs 16:27).

DAY 7

Read and meditate on the entire chapter of Nehemiah 7.

- ➤ Notice that those who serve in the house of God are never forgotten.
- ➤ In this chapter Nehemiah registers the names of all those who have contributed to the work and the building of God's wall.
- ➤ Others were greatly rewarded for what they did and some were promoted and placed in higher positions in life.
- ➤ It is also my prayer that this fasting and prayer will bring you promotion and upliftment in all your life endeavors.
- ➤ May God remember you and bring you into a place of honor and remembrance before His throne, in Jesus name.

LOG-ON: Morning Prayers

Enter and make these declarations over your life and church (pray each point at least 5 minutes; this is will give you a total of at least 60minutes in morning prayer). Pray this prayer for your personal growth:

1. Under the covering of the Superior Blood of Jesus the Christ, Empower me, O Lord, to be non-conformed to worldly vanities, in the name of Jesus.

2. Under the covering of the Superior Blood of Jesus the Christ, Empower me, O Lord, to be transformed by a renewed mind, in the name of Jesus.

3. Under the covering of the Superior Blood of Jesus the Christ, Empower me, O Lord, to be covered in the entire armor of God, in the name of Jesus.

4. Under the covering of the Superior Blood of Jesus the Christ, Empower me, O Lord, to shine as a never-dimmed light, in the name of Jesus.

5. Under the covering of the Superior Blood of Jesus the Christ, Empower me, O Lord, to show holiness in all my ways, in the name of Jesus.

6. Under the covering of the Superior Blood of Jesus the Christ, Let no evil soil my thoughts, words and hands, O Lord, in the name of Jesus.

7. Under the covering of the Superior Blood of Jesus the Christ, My Father, let my affection be in heaven, in the name of Jesus.

8. Under the covering of the Superior Blood of Jesus the Christ, Father, let me view all things in the mirror of eternity, in the name of Jesus.

9. Under the covering of the Superior Blood of Jesus the Christ, Let all my communications be ordered according to Thy wisdom, in the name of Jesus.

10. Under the covering of the Superior Blood of Jesus the Christ, If my life should end today, let this be my best day, O Lord, in the name of Jesus.

11. Under the covering of the Superior Blood of Jesus the Christ, O Lord, enlarge my soul to contain the fullness of holiness, in the name of Jesus.

12. Under the covering of the Superior Blood of Jesus the Christ, O Lord, wrap my life in divine love, in the name of Jesus.

LOG-OFF: Evening Prayers

Enter and make these declarations over your life and church (pray each point at least 5 minutes; this is will give you a total of at least 60minutes in evening prayer). Pray this prayer for your personal growth:

1. Under the covering of the Superior Blood of Jesus the Christ, Teach me, O Lord, to use Your gifts wisely, in Jesus' name.
2. Under the covering of the Superior Blood of Jesus the Christ, O Lord, forgive me for imagining that I can work independently of You, in the name of Jesus.
3. Under the covering of the Superior Blood of Jesus the Christ, O Lord, forgive me for living and acting as I please with no thought of the consequence, in the name of Jesus.
4. Under the covering of the Superior Blood of Jesus the Christ, O God, guide me in my walk in life, in the name of Jesus.
5. Under the covering of the Superior Blood of Jesus the Christ, Father, come as the dove, the fire and the wind and empower my life, in the name of Jesus.
6. Under the covering of the Superior Blood of Jesus the Christ, O Lord, save me from becoming complacent, in Jesus' name.
7. Under the covering of the Superior Blood of Jesus the Christ, Help us, O lord, to recognize the destructive consequences of my sinfulness, in the name of Jesus.

8. Under the covering of the Superior Blood of Jesus the Christ, Father, give me true humility and true lowliness of heart, in Jesus' name.
9. Under the covering of the Superior Blood of Jesus the Christ, Father, give me humility to accept my faults, in the name of Jesus.
10. Under the covering of the Superior Blood of Jesus the Christ, Teach me to show Your love to people, in the name of Jesus.
11. Under the covering of the Superior Blood of Jesus the Christ, Help me, Lord, to measure time, not by my standards, but by Your standard, in the name of Jesus.
12. Under the covering of the Superior Blood of Jesus the Christ, Our Father, let all division, discord, hatred, death and destruction in my life, be arrested, in the name of Jesus.

DAY 8

Intercessory Prayer

On this day, you'll enlist with Heaven on behalf of the Earth to be an intercessor for Church crisis. You'll devote this whole day praying for the topic indicated in the crisis. As you intercede on behalf of the church and the world, may Heaven speedily answer your personal prayer request. May Almighty God do for you, even as you pray for the pastors of the church.

INTERCESSOR:

TIME:

TOPIC: **Churchlessness or Church Decline –
Give Us A Revival**

PROBLEM:

Most of the statistics tell us that nearly 50% of Americans have no church home. In the 1980s, membership in the church dropped by almost 10%. In the 1990s, it worsened by another 12% drop—some denominations reporting a 40% drop in their membership. Now, over half way through the first decade of the 21st century, we are seeing the figures drop even more!

What is Going on with the Church in America?

The United States Census Bureau Records give some startling statistics, backed by denominational reports and the Assemblies of God U.S. Missions:

- o Every year more than 4000 churches close their doors, compared to just over 1000 new church starts!

- o There were about 4,500 new churches started between 1990 and 2000, with a twenty year average of nearly 1000 a year.

- o Every year, 2.7 million church members fall into inactivity. This translates into the realization that people are leaving the church. From our research, we have found that they are leaving as hurting and wounded victims— of some kind of abuse, disillusionment, or just plain neglect!

- o From 1990 to 2000, the combined membership of all Protestant denominations in the USA declined by almost 5 million members (9.5 percent), while the US population increased by 24 million (11 percent).

- o At the turn of the last century (1900), there was a ratio of 27 churches per 10,000 people, as compared to the close of this century (2000), where we have 11 churches per

10,000 people in America! What has happened?

o Given the declining numbers and closures of churches as compared to new church starts, there should have been over 38,000 new churches commissioned to keep up with the population growth.

o The United States now ranks third (3rd), following China and India in the number of people who are not professing Christians. In other words, the U.S. is becoming an ever increasing "un-reached people group."

o Half of all churches in the US did not add any new members to their ranks in the last two years.

DECLINE:

· 22% of Americans "frequently" attended church in 1992; this includes Orthodox, Evangelical, and Protestant churches. (The reason why the other research is variant is due to how they ask the questions. I sought frequency over just attendance. I deem frequency as at least 2 times a <u>month</u> as opposed to two to three times a <u>year</u> as indicated by other statistical research.)

· 20.5% of Americans "frequently" attended church in 1995.

- 19% of Americans "frequently" attended church in 1999.

- 18.0% of Americans "frequently" attended in church in 2002.

Statistics tell us that 42% to 50% of all churches in America have a congregation of between 100 and 300 members, and 20% of American churches have fewer than 100 members. This is factoring in the mega church trend.

YOUR DUTY: Using the Spiritual Mapping statistics provided above and from any further research, with our Prophetic Intercession Guidelines, pray that the LORD of the Harvest will visit the dead state of our churches, and give us a reviving in this, our calamity. Pray for the latter rain; conviction in the pulpit and pews.

SCRIPTURES ON THE PROMISE: Matthew 16:18; Matthew 9:37-38; Acts 4:12; Ezek. 34:26; 2 Chron. 7:14-15; Psalm 85:6; Isa. 62:1; Isa. 63: 15-19; Dan.9: 1-19; Ezra 9: 6-15; Psalm 60: 1-12; Hab.3:2.

COVENANTED PROMISE: Haggai 2:9 and John 14:12.

CHAPTER 4

WEEK II: I Wept

*And it came to pass, when I heard these words, that I ... **wept** ... **before** the God of heaven.*

– Nehemiah 1:4

4

WEEK TWO – I Wept

We continue the Second Part of the Fasting by meditating on the second thing Nehemiah did as he inquired on the state of Jerusalem before God. As previously discussed, the book opens with this staggering statement from Nehemiah:

> *As soon as I heard these words*
> *I sat down and **wept** and*
> *mourned for days, and I*
> *continued fasting and praying*
> *before the God of heaven –*
> *Nehemiah 1:4*

Nehemiah did five things:
1. I sat down
2. **I wept**
3. I mourned for days
4. I continued fasting
5. I prayed before the God of heaven

During this week of the Fasting, we will enter the next dimension in prayer called **Travailing Prayer or Liquid Prayer.** This is a prayer washed in tears, groaning, wailing, lamenting and agonizing before God.

What is travail and how can it be called a dimension of prayer?

Truthfully, it's not spoken of much in churches. The dictionary calls it *hard or agonizing labor, toil as in childbirth, deep distress or anguish encountered in achievement.* Sometimes (as we'll see) it's not a pretty sight, except maybe to God. Most Christians don't encounter travail because we do not initiate it; God initiates it.

Consider Jeremiah. He served as a prophet to the nation of Israel while they played the harlot with false gods, when God's judgment finally fell. He was there when *"Nebuchadnezzar king of Babylon came, he and all his army, against Jerusalem, camped against it and built a siege wall all around it."* (Jeremiah 52:4). Jeremiah had warned the people it was coming but they rejected him. Still, when Jerusalem fell, he didn't gloat. Rather, he was devastated and prayed for mercy even though he knew none was coming.

Jeremiah is known as the weeping prophet and for good reason. He is a good picture for us of what travail looks like. *"My soul, my soul! I am in anguish! Oh, my heart!" (Jeremiah 4:19) "Oh that my head were waters and my eyes a fountain of tears, that I might weep day and night for the slain of the daughter of my people!"* (Jeremiah 9:1). *"My heart is broken within me, all my bones tremble; I have become like a drunken man, even like a man overcome with wine."* (Jeremiah 23:9).

After the demise of Jerusalem, Jeremiah wrote a soul scorching lament in which he says, *"For these things I weep; my eyes run down with water; because far from me is a comforter, One who restores my soul. My children are desolate because the enemy has prevailed."* (Lamentations 1:16).

I like to call travail, liquid prayer because there are almost never any words—no petitions—no pleadings—no claiming or declaring. Instead, there is strong emotion poured out in weeping, wailing and groanings. *"In the same way the Spirit also helps our weakness; for we do not know how to pray as we should, but the Spirit Himself intercedes for us with groanings too deep for words." (*Romans 8:26). That passage is often used to describe praying in the spirit or praying in tongues, but I think it more accurately describes travail or praying with agonizing tears and sobs.

At times God calls us to weep. (Eccl. 3:4). This is His call to empathy, to vicarious intercessory identification with others. At such times, we must be sure to pray "us" prayers and not "them" prayers. We must identify with those in need, rather than condemn and accuse. Instead of praying, "Lord, forgive them for being so cold," we should pray, "Lord, forgive us as a church for being so cold. Help us to be more loving, help us to pray more, help us to be more effective for You."

How Travail Works – Weeping in Prayer

Let's talk about how travail usually works. When a spirit of travail comes to you, it totally bypasses your mind and intellect. When you reach this dimension of prayer you go beyond your natural self. Your prayers pass the stage of reason, planning, and strategy. This dimension of prayer is activated by the Holy Spirit. You enter the stage where there are no words to articulate your prayer and you are so burdened with the situation that all you can do is sob with uncontrollable tears. The Bible calls it "groaning too deep for words." Have you ever gotten to that point in your prayer life, where words will not do? It is as if God pours into you, a willing partner, His own emotions about an issue so you then become a point of contact on the earth for God's will to be worked through. *"Your kingdom come. Your will be done, on earth as it is in heaven."* (Matthew 6:10).

Response

Have you ever felt such a call to liquid prayer or praying with groaning? How did you respond? When it happens for the first time, it's common to feel some hesitation or even embarrassment, especially if you have no experience or teaching along these lines. Before resisting though, it is good to remember who drew you to such deep intercession. God produces the burden as He may wish to accomplish something very special through you. It is a privilege to be part of it.

If you have never personally experienced travail, have you ever witnessed it? Here again, the right response can help to support it and the wrong one can short-circuit God's purposes. I've seen people become distressed when someone else is in travail and try to shut it down by shushing the person or comforting them as if they are personally in distress. This distraction sometimes diminishes the prayer's fullness.

The best response to travail is to quietly pray in the spirit, perhaps with a gentle hand resting on their shoulder. Or, withdraw from the area and leave them to finish what God has started. If others approach and seem concerned, explain what is happening and ask them to leave or sit quietly and pray also. The one who is travailing is perfectly aware of what is going on around them but they need to have the freedom to carry their prayer to completion.

One who has experienced travail has experienced a deep connection to God's heart. That one has felt what God feels and knows that He is a God of very intense emotions. Should this type of prayer come knocking at your door, will you open wide?

Nehemiah opens his petition with soul travail – I said, when I heard these things I wept. How about you? This kind of weeping in prayer is not carnal, it's not bursting in tears because a matter or a situation hurts you. This dimension of prayer is truly spiritual; it is God initiated and provoked in you. You can't control it. You can feel you're in connection with God and you're expressing yourself, though you can't form words to express it. Deep tears or groans in prayer is a spiritual communication that can accelerate the results of your prayer request if you remain tuned with God.

In this devotional, I invite you to desire a spiritual experience of groaning before God that is too deep for words to express.

DAY 9

Scripture Reading: Nehemiah 8 (read entire chapter).

"Those who sow in tears will reap with songs of joy. He who goes out weeping, carrying seed to sow, will return with songs of joy, carrying sheaves with him." (Psa. 126:5-6).

Tears are precious in the sight of God when they are tears of longing, shed in intercession, or tears of joy as you praise God for answered prayer. The Son of God knows what it means to weep in prayer. The shortest verse in the Bible, *"Jesus wept"* (John 11:35), not only speaks volumes about the love and compassion of Jesus; it also explains the relation of tears to the intercession of Jesus. He who weeps *with* us wept *for* us as He wrestled with the powers of darkness in the Garden. (Heb. 5:7).

Let us make very clear that we are not talking about tears of self-pity. Such tears can be basically carnal. They may give relief from tension, for "a good cry" often helps the mood of a discouraged or depressed person. However, recurring tears of self-pity give no testimony to spiritual depth or power. We are here discussing the power of tears resulting from deep spiritual desire.

You should never be ashamed of tears shed in loving intercession. In fact, they testify to God of the depth of your identity with those for whom you intercede, the intensity of longing which underlies your intercession, and serve as a testimony of the Holy Spirit praying through you. Tears add a personal and private dimension of poignancy and power.

Such weeping intercession is much more likely to occur when you are alone with God. Normally, our private prayer can be more deep and intense than our public prayer. Tears are so intensely personal that the praying soul can weep more naturally and freely when only God is the witness to the tears. It is possible, however, to have a weeping spirit even when no literal tear runs down your cheek. God looks on your heart above all else. (1 Sam. 16:7).

Your tears, like your words, are very important. However, God sees and knows you as you really are. (2 Sam. 7:20; John 21:17). God knows the secret depths of your longing even better than you can express it. By deeply identifying with those for whom you pray, seek to deepen your heart's cry to God. Do not however seek to produce outward tears. That would be hypocritical. Welcome the tears when the Holy Spirit gives them, but seek only to feel in your innermost heart the depth of yearning, which the Spirit feels.

LOG-ON: Morning Prayer

Enter and make these declarations over your life and church (pray each point at least 5 minutes; this is will give you a total of at least 60 minutes in morning prayer). Pray this prayer for your personal growth:

1. Under the covering of the Superior Blood of Jesus the Christ, Turn again my captivity, O Lord, as the streams of the south, in the name of Jesus.
2. Under the covering of the Superior Blood of Jesus the Christ, Heal my backsliding, O Lord, and take not Your Holy Spirit from me, in the name of Jesus.
3. Under the covering of the Superior Blood of Jesus the Christ, Father, let me see Your glory in the mirror of Your word and be changed by it, in the name of Jesus.
4. Under the covering of the Superior Blood of Jesus the Christ, Empower me, O Lord, to daily deny worldly and dishonorable affections and desires, in the name of Jesus.
5. Under the covering of the Superior Blood of Jesus the Christ, Father, let Your voice be my only law and Your smile, my only reward, in the name of Jesus.
6. Under the covering of the Superior Blood of Jesus the Christ, Hold me by Thy hand, O Lord, and make my crooked places straight, in the name of Jesus.
7. Under the covering of the Superior Blood of Jesus the Christ, O LORD, Let Your name be honored in my conduct and conversation, in the name of Jesus.

8. Under the covering of the Superior Blood of Jesus the Christ, My Father, lead me to the rock that is higher than I, in Jesus' name.
9. Under the covering of the Superior Blood of Jesus the Christ, In the shadow of Your wings, O Lord, I will make my refuge, in the name of Jesus.
10. Under the covering of the Superior Blood of Jesus the Christ, O God, arise and sustain me by Your strong arm, in the name of Jesus.
11. Under the covering of the Superior Blood of Jesus the Christ, My Father, clean my feet, hands, and lips from the stains of the flesh and spirit, in the name of Jesus.
12. Under the covering of the Superior Blood of Jesus the Christ, O Lord, teach me to live a holy life in the fear of the Lord, in the name of Jesus.

LOG-OFF: Evening Prayers

Enter and make these declarations over your life and church (pray each point at least 5 minutes; this is will give you a total of at least 60 minutes in evening prayer). Pray this prayer for your personal growth:

1. Under the covering of the Superior Blood of Jesus the Christ, O Lord, give me encouragement in the time of despair, in Jesus' name.
2. Under the covering of the Superior Blood of Jesus the Christ, O Lord, give me guidance in the time of uncertainty, in the name of Jesus.
3. Under the covering of the Superior Blood of Jesus the Christ, Help me, Lord, to draw closer to You, day by day, in the name of Jesus.
4. Under the covering of the Superior Blood of Jesus the Christ, Father, empower me to hear Your voice and discern Your will, in the name of Jesus.
5. Under the covering of the Superior Blood of Jesus the Christ, Father, save me from becoming over-familiar with You, in Jesus' name.
6. Under the covering of the Superior Blood of Jesus the Christ, The God who does more than I can ever ask or think, manifest Your power in my life, in the name of Jesus.
7. Under the covering of the Superior Blood of Jesus the Christ, Teach me, Lord, to seek Your will and pursue what is right, in the name of Jesus.
8. Under the covering of the Superior Blood of Jesus the Christ, Help me, Lord, to love You without reservation, in Jesus' name.

9. Under the covering of the Superior Blood of Jesus the Christ, O God, challenge and confront me through Your word and meet with me in prayers, in the name of Jesus.
10. Under the covering of the Superior Blood of Jesus the Christ, I release myself from the fears and anxieties that weigh me down, in the name of Jesus.
11. Under the covering of the Superior Blood of Jesus the Christ, I release myself from powers destroying my confidence and undermining my happiness, in the name of Jesus.
12. Under the covering of the Superior Blood of Jesus the Christ, Almighty God, by Your power, teach me to see with Your eyes, in the name of Jesus.

DAY 10

Scripture Reading: Nehemiah 9 (read entire chapter).

As we enter the 10th day of our Fasting, we must seek to meditate on what it means to "Weep before the LORD" as Nehemiah did. Many of God's chosen servants have prayed with groaning and tears until the petition was granted. Observe these ones:

Job testified, *"Have I not wept for those in trouble? Has not my soul grieved for the poor?"* (Job 30:25). Moses and others of the children of Israel wept over the sin of their people. (Numbers 25:6). David testified as to how he wept and fasted for God's people. (Psa. 69:10). Isaiah wept for the need of his people. (Isaiah 16:9). God told King Josiah: *"Because your heart was responsive and you humbled yourself before the Lord...and because you tore your robes and wept in My presence, I have heard you, declares the Lord."* (2 Kings 22:19).

When Ezra wept for his people, they began to weep and pray also. (Ezra 10:1). Nehemiah *"sat down and wept [for*

Jerusalem]. For some days I mourned and fasted and prayed before the God of heaven." (Neh. 1:4).

Jeremiah was known as the weeping prophet because of the great prayer burden he carried for his people. *"Since my people are crushed, I am crushed; I mourn...Oh, that my head were a spring of water and my eyes a fountain of tears! I would weep day and night for...my people"* (Jeremiah 8:21; 9:1). *"If you do not listen, I will weep in secret because of your pride; my eyes will weep bitterly, overflowing with tears"* (Jeremiah 13:17). *"Let my eyes overflow with tears night and day without ceasing; for my virgin daughter – my people – has suffered a grievous wound, a crushing blow."* (Jeremiah 14:17). *"My eyes fail from weeping, I am in torment within, my heart is poured out on the ground because my people are destroyed."* (Lamentation 2:11). *"Streams of tears flow from my eyes because my people are destroyed. My eyes will flow unceasingly, without relief, until the Lord looks down from heaven and sees. What I see brings grief to my soul."* (Lamentation 3:48-51).

Paul, the great missionary apostle, was also known for his ministry of tears. *"I wrote you out of great distress and anguish of heart and with many tears."* (2 Corinthians 2:4). *"You know how I lived the whole time I was with you...I served the Lord with great humility and with tears."* (Acts 20:18-19). *"Remember that for three years I never stopped warning each of you night and day with tears."* (Acts 20:31).

Truly, the act of weeping before God has been a chosen weapon by some of God's choicest servants. You should not be ashamed to join the company of these servants.

LOG-ON: Morning Prayer

Enter and make these declarations over your life and church (pray each point at least 5 minutes; this is will give you a total of at least 60 minutes in morning prayer). Pray this prayer for your personal growth:

1. Under the covering of the Superior Blood of Jesus the Christ, Father, give me a loving and thankful heart, in Jesus' name.
2. Under the covering of the Superior Blood of Jesus the Christ, Make me a blessing, O Lord, to those with whom I come in contact, in the name of Jesus.
3. Under the covering of the Superior Blood of Jesus the Christ, Keep me away, O Lord, from all that would grieve Your Holy Spirit, in the name of Jesus.
4. Under the covering of the Superior Blood of Jesus the Christ, Help me, O Lord, to remove my gaze from lusting after impurities and unholy desires, and focus on Your desires, in the name of Jesus.
5. Under the covering of the Superior Blood of Jesus the Christ, Help me, O Lord, not to focus on the waves and the wind, but on the face of JESUS, in the name of Jesus.
6. Under the covering of the Superior Blood of Jesus the Christ, Help me, O Lord, never to complain about Your discipleship, in the name of Jesus.
7. Under the covering of the Superior Blood of Jesus the Christ, My Father, take the burden I cannot bear

and wipe the tears I cannot keep back, in the name of Jesus.

8. Under the covering of the Superior Blood of Jesus the Christ, I shall not fail under Your discipleship, O Lord, in Jesus' name.

9. Under the covering of the Superior Blood of Jesus the Christ, Blessed Holy Spirit, give me joy that is unspeakable, in Jesus' name.

10. Under the covering of the Superior Blood of Jesus the Christ, Blessed Holy Spirit, give me love that passes knowledge, in Jesus' name.

11. Under the covering of the Superior Blood of Jesus the Christ, Blessed Holy Spirit, give me peace beyond understanding, in the name of Jesus.

12. Under the covering of the Superior Blood of Jesus the Christ, O Lord my God, graciously draw near to me and cover my head when I am in trouble, in the name of Jesus.

LOG-OFF: Evening Prayers

Enter and make these declarations over your life and church (pray each point at least 5 minutes; this is will give you a total of at least 60 minutes in evening prayer). Pray this prayer for your personal growth:

1. Under the covering of the Superior Blood of Jesus the Christ, Fountain of life, spring up in me, in the name of Jesus.
2. Under the covering of the Superior Blood of Jesus the Christ, Light of life, Jesus Christ, illuminate my life, in Jesus' name.
3. Under the covering of the Superior Blood of Jesus the Christ, Overshadow me with the comfort and peace that no one can take away, in the name of Jesus.
4. Under the covering of the Superior Blood of Jesus the Christ, Help me, O Lord, to take up my cross and follow You, in Jesus' name.
5. Under the covering of the Superior Blood of Jesus the Christ, O Lord, support me with Your mighty power and enable me to become more than a conqueror, in the name of Jesus.
6. Under the covering of the Superior Blood of Jesus the Christ, Give me the grace, O God, to be steadfast, unmovable and strong, in the name of Jesus.
7. Under the covering of the Superior Blood of Jesus the Christ, My Father, write Your law upon my heart, in Jesus' name.

8. Under the covering of the Superior Blood of Jesus the Christ, Father, let the leaves of the tree of life be for my health, in Jesus' name.

9. Under the covering of the Superior Blood of Jesus the Christ, Father, let Your peace settle down upon my soul, in the name of Jesus.

10. Under the covering of the Superior Blood of Jesus the Christ, My Father, make me sensitive to Your voice, in Jesus' name.

11. Under the covering of the Superior Blood of Jesus the Christ, I shall not have fellowship with the works of darkness, in Jesus' name.

12. Under the covering of the Superior Blood of Jesus the Christ, My Father, let me live in the spirit of prayer all my days, in the name of Jesus.

DAY 11

Scripture Reading: *Nehemiah 10 (read and meditate on entire chapter).*

God Calls Us to Pray with Tears

God called through the prophet Joel, *"Return to Me with all your heart, with fasting and weeping and mourning."* (Joel 2:12). He calls Christian leaders to pray with tears for their people: *"Let the priests, who minister before the Lord, weep between the temple porch and the altar. Let them say, 'Spare Your people, O Lord'...Why should they say among the peoples, 'Where is their God?'"* (2:17). God knows and records our tears: *"List my tears on Your scroll – are they not in Your record?"* (Psa. 56:8). Our day is similar to that faced by Isaiah. *"The Lord, the Lord Almighty, called you on that day to weep."* (Isa. 22:12).

It will take more than tears to make prayer effective; but a burdened heart, a soul crying out to God, is the very essence of intercession. It is a spiritual crime to be calloused while the world goes to hell. It is spiritually criminal to pray casually, dry-eyed and burden-less, while a world is in sin and pain. It is Christ-like for your heart to weep with those who weep. (Rom. 12:15). It is Christ-like for you to be so filled with loving compassion that you pray with tears for those broken, fettered, and destroyed by sin.

Prayer is not recreational or arbitrary for the Christian. Prayer is the very business of Christ's kingdom. Prayer is joining with God the brokenhearted Father, Christ the weeping High Priest, and the tender, interceding Holy Spirit, by sharing their heartbeat and bearing with them the same burdens which they carry in their loving hearts.

To pray with tears is to make an eternal investment. To pray with tears is to sow your tears with eternal harvest. No tear shed in burdened intercession for others is ever forgotten by God, unrecorded, or in vain. Intercession watered with your tears is one of the most powerful forms of prayer known. As surely as God is in heaven, *"Those who sow in tears will reap with songs of joy. He who goes out weeping, carrying seed to sow, will return with songs of joy, carrying sheaves with him."* (Psa. 126:5-6).

LOG-ON: Morning Prayers

Enter and make these declarations over your life and church (pray each point at least 5 minutes; this is will give you a total of at least 60 minutes in morning prayer). Pray this prayer for your personal growth:

1. Under the covering of the Superior Blood of Jesus the Christ, Heavenly Father, fence me around with Your protecting care, in the name of Jesus.
2. Under the covering of the Superior Blood of Jesus the Christ, Father, empower me to finish my course with joy and receive the crown of life, in the name of Jesus.
3. Under the covering of the Superior Blood of Jesus the Christ, My Lord, be the physician of my soul, in the name of Jesus.
4. Under the covering of the Superior Blood of Jesus the Christ, Father, heal all the diseases of my soul, in the name of Jesus.
5. Under the covering of the Superior Blood of Jesus the Christ, Father, lighten my heart with the knowledge of Your truth, in the name of Jesus.
6. Under the covering of the Superior Blood of Jesus the Christ, Purify me, O Lord, by the fire of Your Holy Spirit, in the name of Jesus.
7. Under the covering of the Superior Blood of Jesus the Christ, Heavenly Father, wash my life with pure water, in the name of Jesus.

8. Under the covering of the Superior Blood of Jesus the Christ, Holy Ghost, help me to live as an uncluttered man, in Jesus' name.
9. Under the covering of the Superior Blood of Jesus the Christ, Feed me, O lord, with Your flesh and blood according to Your power, in the name of Jesus.
10. Under the covering of the Superior Blood of Jesus the Christ, true Vine of God, abide in me by fire, in the name of Jesus.
11. Under the covering of the Superior Blood of Jesus the Christ, Lord, deliver me from the terror of the night, in the name of Jesus.
12. Under the covering of the Superior Blood of Jesus the Christ, Empower me, O Lord, to lean on Your strength, in Jesus' name.

LOG-OFF: Evening Prayers

Enter and make these declarations over your life and church (pray each point at least 5 minutes; this is will give you a total of at least 60 minutes in evening prayer). Pray this prayer for your personal growth:

1. Under the covering of the Superior Blood of Jesus the Christ, Minister nourishment to my soul, in the name of Jesus.
2. Under the covering of the Superior Blood of Jesus the Christ, My Father, do not let sin have dominion over my life, in Jesus' name.
3. Under the covering of the Superior Blood of Jesus the Christ, When I am fiercely tempted, O Lord, do not let me yield, in the name of Jesus.
4. Under the covering of the Superior Blood of Jesus the Christ, Be the Alpha and Omega of every moment of my life, in Jesus' name.
5. Under the covering of the Superior Blood of Jesus the Christ, Let the fire of Your love consume every sinful desire in me, in the name of Jesus.
6. Under the covering of the Superior Blood of Jesus the Christ, Keep me, O Lord, in quietness of spirit, in the name of Jesus.
7. Under the covering of the Superior Blood of Jesus the Christ, Help me, O Lord, to make others glad, in the name of Jesus.
8. Under the covering of the Superior Blood of Jesus the Christ, Help me to serve You in opening blind eyes and turning men and women from darkness to light, in the name of Jesus.

9. Under the covering of the Superior Blood of Jesus the Christ, Father, Let Your power work through my hands, in Jesus' name.
10. Under the covering of the Superior Blood of Jesus the Christ, Give me uncommon wisdom to enable me know what I ought to know, in the name of Jesus.
11. Under the covering of the Superior Blood of Jesus the Christ, Give me grace, O Lord, so that I will never grieve Your Holy Spirit, in the name of Jesus.
12. Under the covering of the Superior Blood of Jesus the Christ, Power of wandering from the church, perish from my life, in the name of Jesus.

DAY 12

Scripture Reading: *Nehemiah 11 – read and meditate on entire chapter*

We should weep because humanity has forsaken God!

The nations have forgotten God. (Psa. 9:17). They do not want to retain the knowledge of God. (Rom. 1:28). They show contempt for God's constant kindness, tolerance and patience. (Rom. 2:4). Often they are hardened by God's judgments and their reaping of what they have sown. (Rom. 2:5; Rev. 16:21). We should weep for our world: "Lord, forgive our wayward race!"

Why should we not weep when satanic inspired legislations are passed in our Congress every year? Christianity needs a heart with compassion to cry for a world that is laughing it's way to hell.

LOG-ON: Morning Prayer

Enter and make these declarations over your life and church (pray each point at least 5 minutes; this is will give you a total of at least 60 minutes in morning prayer). Pray this prayer for your personal growth:

1. Under the covering of the Superior Blood of Jesus the Christ, Lord Jesus, thank You for giving Your Church, Evangelists to perfect us.
2. Under the covering of the Superior Blood of Jesus the Christ, Lord Jesus, thank You for giving Your Church, Pastors to perfect us.
3. Under the covering of the Superior Blood of Jesus the Christ, Lord Jesus, thank You for giving Your Church, Teachers to perfect us.
4. Under the covering of the Superior Blood of Jesus the Christ, O God, I thank You for giving me a tongue that is like the best silver.
5. Under the covering of the Superior Blood of Jesus the Christ, O God, I thank You for You are a covenant-keeping God.
6. Under the covering of the Superior Blood of Jesus the Christ, O God, I thank You for You give mercy and peace to all who keep Your covenant.
7. Under the covering of the Superior Blood of Jesus the Christ, O God, I thank You for You are not a man who lies – You will do what You have promised.
8. Under the covering of the Superior Blood of Jesus the Christ, O God, I thank You for You are not slack concerning Your promises.

9. Under the covering of the Superior Blood of Jesus the Christ, Father of Truth, I thank You for You have promised never to leave me.

10. Under the covering of the Superior Blood of Jesus the Christ, Father of Truth, I thank You for You have promised never to forsake me.

11. Under the covering of the Superior Blood of Jesus the Christ, Father of Truth, I thank You for You have promised to deliver me.

12. Under the covering of the Superior Blood of Jesus the Christ, Father of Truth, I thank You for You have promised to be my sun and shield.

LOG-OFF: Evening Prayer

Enter and make these declarations over your life and church (pray each point at least 5 minutes; this is will give you a total of at least 60 minutes in evening prayer). Pray this prayer for your personal growth:

1. Under the covering of the Superior Blood of the Living Christ, O Lord! I lift up my eyes to your Holy Hills, where my help comes from; And I declare today, incline your ear unto me, and haste your help toward me in this my trouble, in Jesus' name – PRAY...

2. Under the covering of the Superior Blood of the Living Christ, I confess and believe that you are the creator of the Heavens and the Earth, you control

the affairs of men and the universe, I now submit myself for Divine control and supervision. Pilot my life O Lord, and lead me to the still waters, in Jesus' name – PRAY…

3. Under the covering of the Superior Blood of the Living Christ, You kept Israel, and did not slumber nor sleep, order my feet not to be moved in this my distress; strengthen me, uphold me, and cause any demonic satellite devices watching over my life to catch afire now, in Jesus' name – PRAY…

4. Under the covering of the Superior Blood of the Living Christ, O Lord, I submit that you are the keeper of my life. Now, cause any networks of demonic eyes, crystal balls, magic mirrors, and sorcery monitoring my life to be destroyed by Your consuming fire now, in Jesus' name – PRAY…

5. Under the covering of the Superior Blood of the Living Christ, Any demonic influence that works with the energy of the sun to destroy my life and to smite me by day; obey the Word of the Lord, and terminate now, in Jesus' name. PRAY…

6. Under the covering of the Superior Blood of the Living Christ, Any occult mysticism that employs the power of the moon to interrupt my destiny, receive fire now and face utter destruction in Jesus' name. PRAY…

7. Under the covering of the Superior Blood of the Living Christ, I Command the Sun and the Moon to favor my cause, and work in my favor, in Jesus' name. (Isaiah 45:11) - PRAY…

8. Under the covering of the Superior Blood of the Living Christ, I confess and believe that I am shielded, protected, and defended against any

demonic assaults, counterattacks, charms, curses and divinations and enchantments in Jesus' name. (3x)- PRAY...

9. O Lord, preserve my soul from soul-robbers and demonic soul-ties. I lock myself under thy control, steer my going in and my coming in from this time forth and forever more, in Jesus' name. PRAY...

10. Under the covering of the Superior Blood of the Living Christ, O Lord, I boldly confess and believe that You are my hiding place; you will protect me from trouble and surround me with songs of deliverance, in Jesus' name. PRAY...

11. Under the covering of the Superior Blood of the Living Christ, My LORD protect me and preserve my life. Bless me in this land and do not surrender me to the desire of my foes, in Jesus' name. PRAY...

12. Under the covering of the Superior Blood of the Living Christ, I acknowledge that this year, no harm will befall me, no disaster will come near my tent, in Jesus' name. PRAY...

DAY 13

Scripture Reading: Nehemiah 12 – read and meditate on the entire chapter.

We should weep because sin is multiplying!

Evil people are going from bad to worse, deceiving and being deceived. (2 Tim. 3:13). The sins listed in Second Timothy 3:1-5 are all too evident: loving self rather than loving God, boastfulness, pride, abusiveness, disobedience to parents, ungratefulness, unholiness, unloveliness, unforgiveness, slander, lack of self-control, brutality, despising the good, treachery, rashness, conceit, love of pleasure more than love of God.

All these combined with the gross sins of sexual perversion, rape and pornography, have hardened our national conscience. Crime has escalated. Terrorism, sadism, and calculated cruelty have reached unimaginable proportions. War is ever more terrible, and peace seems constantly precarious. Man seems on the verge of destroying himself. How can we but weep: "Lord, have mercy on our sinful race!"

LOG-ON: Morning Prayer

Enter and make these declarations over your life and church (pray each point at least 5 minutes; this is will give you a total of at least 60 minutes in morning prayer).

1. Under the covering of the Superior Blood of the Living Christ, I confess and receive cleansing for any iniquities and transgressions connected to me, in Jesus' name.
2. Under the covering of the Superior Blood of the Living Christ, Oh LORD, wash me from any sins that are choking my life path, in Jesus' name.
3. Under the covering of the Superior Blood of the Living Christ, I take coverage under the mercy of His speaking Blood against any power crying for my prosecution, in Jesus' name.
4. Under the covering of the Superior Blood of the Living Christ, I silence every voice of the Accuser against my life now, in Jesus' name.
5. Under the covering of the Superior Blood of the Living Christ, By the power of the risen Christ, of whom I am, and to whom I belong, I condemn and eject out of my body, soul, and spirit, any venom of Satan and his cohort now in Jesus' name. (3x)
6. Under the covering of the Superior Blood of the Living Christ, I boldly confess and declare that neither death nor life, neither angels nor demons, neither the present nor the future, nor any powers under and above the heavens shall be able to separate me from the covenanted love of Christ Jesus.

7. Under the covering of the Superior Blood of the Living Christ, O Lord of my Salvation, surround me now with the gates of praise, and cover me with the canopy of favor this year in Jesus' name. (3x).

8. Under the covering of the Superior Blood of the Living Christ, I boldly renounce, and utterly delete any demonic dream inserted in my body, soul, and spirit since I was born. I command you to be permanently deleted now, in Jesus name.

9. Under the covering of the Superior Blood of the Living Christ, I decree and declare by the consuming sulfuric fire of the Holy Spirit, that any evil calendar with my name on it shall catch fire now, in Jesus' name.

10. Under the covering of the Superior Blood of the Living Christ, Any occult and witchcraft destruction list with my name on it, terminate by fire now, in Jesus' name.

11. Under the covering of the Superior Blood of the Living Christ, I delete my name from any evil altars, databases, and network devices. in Jesus name. (3x.)

12. Under the covering of the Superior Blood of the Living Christ, As a validated and authentic child of the Almighty Father, purchased by the Superior Blood of Jesus Christ, and legally adopted into the Heavenly order and heir to the throne of the Kingdom, I petition the throne of my Father to charge His angels to remove any barricades, hindrances, and potholes compressing my progress, my capacity to expand, and diminishing my strength to excel, in Jesus name.

LOG-OFF: Evening Prayers

Enter and make these declarations over your life and church (pray each point at least 5 minutes; this is will give you a total of at least 60 minutes in evening prayer).

1. Under the covering of the Superior Blood of the Living Christ, I declare, the LORD GOD has given me the tongue of those who are instructed to know how to sustain the weary with a word.
2. Under the covering of the Superior Blood of the Living Christ, Lord, let the lifting of my hands, the meditations of my heart, and my spirit-filled tongue be acceptable in your sight.
3. Under the covering of the Superior Blood of the Living Christ, Awaken my ear to listen like those being instructed. Open thou my ear, and I will not be rebellious, I will not retreat in the midst of adversity.
4. Under the covering of the Superior Blood of the Living Christ, I boldly confess and declare, that the LORD GOD will help me, therefore I will not be humiliated.
5. Under the covering of the Superior Blood of the Living Christ, I earnestly confess and declare, Jehovah is near to justify me today. I have set my face like flint, and I know I will not be put to shame.
6. Under the covering of the Superior Blood of the Living Christ, I stand in the mist of the Heavens and the Earth, and declare, who will contend with me? Let us confront each other. Who has a case against me? Let him come near me! In truth the LORD will help me; who is he who will condemn me?

7. Under the covering of the Superior Blood of the Living Christ, I decree by divine edict that my adversaries and their fortress of operation against my life shall wear out like a garment; Ah today! Let a moth devour them, in Jesus' name.

8. Under the covering of the Superior Blood of the Living Christ, LORD, observe the deeds of my adversaries, you know my words were spoken in your presence. Silence now the voice of the Accuser of the Brethren, and reduce and gather them to a dunghill.

9. Under the covering of the Superior Blood of the Living Christ, Any false advertisement and negative commercials against my life, backfire now, in Jesus' name.

10. Under the covering of the Superior Blood of the Living Christ, Now O LORD, become a terror to those who stand against my success and progress; You are my sure refuge in the day of disaster.

11. Under the covering of the Superior Blood of the Living Christ, Let my persecutors be put to shame, but don't let me be put to shame.

12. Under the covering of the Superior Blood of the Living Christ, Oh LORD, Let those that seek my harm be terrified, but don't let me be afraid.

DAY 14

Scripture Reading: Nehemiah 13 – read and meditate on
the entire chapter

We should weep because as a church we are too lifeless and powerless!

We can thank God for the dedicated believers in many
parts of the world, and for what He is doing through them.
We also bless God for what He is doing amongst us here at
Honeywell Baptist Church. But the world has lost its
respect for the Christian church in general, for we do not
bring glory to God as we should.

We have the *"reputation of being alive,"* but all too
often we are spiritually dead. (Rev. 3:1). We lack the
power that should witness to the world of spirituality and
Godliness (2 Tim. 3:5). There is a drifting or departure
from sound doctrine, and false cults are multiplying. (2

Tim. 4:3-4). Too often our spiritual condition is typified by the Laodicean church; we do not realize how lukewarm, pitiful, spiritually impoverished, spiritually blind, and spiritually naked we appear to God. (Rev. 3:17).

What a small percentage of good churches are really characterized by revival, by constant soul-winning by the majority of the membership, and a sacrificial involvement in missionary enterprise. We need to weep for ourselves: "Lord, revive us again!"

LOG-ON: Morning Prayers

Enter and make these declarations over your life and church (pray each point at least 5 minutes; this is will give you a total of at least 60 minutes in morning prayer).

1. Under the covering of the Superior Blood of the Living Christ, Thank You Father for the promise which says, "I will build my church and the gates of hell shall not prevail against it."
2. Under the covering of the Superior Blood of the Living Christ, I ask for forgiveness for every sin causing disunity and powerlessness in the body of Christ.
3. Under the covering of the Superior Blood of the Living Christ, I take authority, over the power of darkness in all its ramifications, in the name of Jesus.
4. Under the covering of the Superior Blood of the Living Christ, I bind and cast out, every spirit causing seduction, false doctrine, deception, hypocrisy, pride and error, in Jesus' name.
5. Under the covering of the Superior Blood of the Living Christ, Every plan and strategy of satan, against the body of Christ, be bound, in the name of Jesus.
6. Under the covering of the Superior Blood of the Living Christ, Every spirit of prayerlessness, discouragement and vainglory in the body of Christ, be bound, in the name of Jesus.
7. Under the covering of the Superior Blood of the Living Christ, Father, let the spirit of brokenness be released upon us, in Jesus' name.

8. Under the covering of the Superior Blood of the Living Christ, I command the works of the flesh, in the lives of the brethren to die, in the name of Jesus.

9. Under the covering of the Superior Blood of the Living Christ, Let the power of the cross and of the Holy Spirit, be released to dethrone flesh in our lives, in the name of Jesus.

10. Under the covering of the Superior Blood of the Living Christ, Let the life of our Lord Jesus Christ, be truly established in the body of Christ, in the name of Jesus.

11. Under the covering of the Superior Blood of the Living Christ, Every power of selfishness, over-ambition and unteachableness, be broken, in the name of Jesus.

12. Under the covering of the Superior Blood of the Living Christ, Father, grant unto the body of Christ, the mind of Christ, a forgiving spirit, tolerance, genuine repentance, understanding, submission, humility, brokenness, watchfulness and the mind to commend others better than ourselves, in the name of Jesus.

LOG-OFF: Evening Prayers

Enter and make these declarations over your life and church (pray each point at least 5 minutes; this is will give you a total of at least 60 minutes in evening prayer).

1. Under the covering of the Superior Blood of the Living Christ, I break down the authority and dominion of satan, over the souls of men, in the name of Jesus.
2. Under the covering of the Superior Blood of the Living Christ, Every spirit holding the souls of men in captivity, I shatter your back-bone, in the name of Jesus.
3. Under the covering of the Superior Blood of the Living Christ, Every covenant, between the souls of men and satan, I dash you to pieces, in the name of Jesus.
4. Under the covering of the Superior Blood of the Living Christ, Let the spirit of steadfastness, consistency, hunger and thirst for the words of God come upon the converts, in the name of Jesus.
5. Under the covering of the Superior Blood of the Living Christ, O Lord, release upon all missionaries and evangelists fresh fire to disgrace territorial spirits, in the name of Jesus.
6. Under the covering of the Superior Blood of the Living Christ, I break the power and the grip of the world, upon the souls of men, in the name of Jesus.
7. Under the covering of the Superior Blood of the Living Christ, I release the spirit of salvation, upon areas that have not been reached by the gospel, in the name of Jesus.

8. Under the covering of the Superior Blood of the Living Christ, O Lord, remove all the hindrances to Your purpose for Christian homes, in the name of Jesus.

9. Under the covering of the Superior Blood of the Living Christ, I command the spirit of quarrel, immorality, unfaithfulness, infirmity, disagreement, misunderstanding and intolerance, to loose their grips upon Christian homes, in the name of Jesus.

10. Under the covering of the Superior Blood of the Living Christ, Let all Christian homes, be a light to the world, and a vehicle of salvation, in the name of Jesus.

11. Under the covering of the Superior Blood of the Living Christ, O God, raise up Esther, Ruth and Deborah in this generation, in the name of Jesus.

12. Under the covering of the Superior Blood of the Living Christ, Every power, destroying joy in my home and local church, be dismantled, in the name of Jesus.

DAY 15

Scripture Reading: *Lamentation 1 – read and meditate on entire chapter*

We should weep because we as God's people are spiritually asleep.

> *"Do this, understanding the present time. The hour has come for you to wake up from your slumber....The night is nearly over; the day is almost here"* (Rom. 13:11-12). It is a shame that we have been sleeping in harvest (Prov. 10:5).

We have largely lost the witnessing, soul-winning passion of the early church. We are upset by blatant sins, but fail to be disturbed by Christians who have never won a soul to Christ, by Christians whose prayer is mostly self-centered and who seldom weep for the world. Earth's largest and whitest harvest since Pentecost is here, and we live a life of "business as usual"; we tend to play church and to treat missions as a mere hobby instead of as the major task of the church.

May God move us to tears: "Lord, awaken me, and stir me and my church again and again!"

"Lord, give us tears as we pray!"

> *"This is why I weep and my eyes overflow with tears. No one is near to comfort me, no one to restore my spirit. My children are destitute because the enemy has prevailed." -* Lamentation 1:16

LOG-ON: Morning Prayers

Enter these declarations and pray one each point for 5 to 10 minutes as time permits.

1. Under the covering of the Superior Blood of the Living Christ, Father, in the name of Jesus, I confess all the sins and iniquities of the land, of our ancestors, of our leaders, and of the people, including, but not limited to violence, rejection of God, corruption, idolatry, robbery, suspicion,

injustice, bitterness, bloody-riots, pogroms, rebellion, conspiracy, shedding of innocent blood, tribal conflicts, child-kidnapping and murder, occultism, mismanagement, negligence.

2. Under the covering of the Superior Blood of the Living Christ, I plead for Your mercy and forgiveness, in the name of Jesus.

3. Under the covering of the Superior Blood of the Living Christ, O Lord, remember our land and redeem it.

4. Under the covering of the Superior Blood of the Living Christ, O Lord, save our land from destruction and judgment.

5. Under the covering of the Superior Blood of the Living Christ, Let Your healing power, begin to operate upon our land, in Jesus' name.

6. Under the covering of the Superior Blood of the Living Christ, Let all forces of darkness, hindering the move of God in this nation, be rendered impotent, in the name of Jesus.

7. Under the covering of the Superior Blood of the Living Christ, I command the spiritual strongman, in charge of this country, to be bound and be disgraced, in the name of Jesus.

8. Under the covering of the Superior Blood of the Living Christ, Let every evil establishment and satanic tree, in this country be uprooted and cast into fire, in the name of Jesus.

9. Under the covering of the Superior Blood of the Living Christ, I come against every spirit of the anti-Christ, working against this nation and I command them to be permanently frustrated, in the name of Jesus.

10. Under the covering of the Superior Blood of the Living Christ, I command the stones of fire from God, to fall upon every national satanic operation and activity, in Jesus' name.
11. Under the covering of the Superior Blood of the Living Christ, Let the desires, plans, devices and expectations of the enemy for this country, be completely frustrated, in Jesus' name.
12. Under the covering of the Superior Blood of the Living Christ, Let every satanic curse on this nation, fall down to the ground and be void, in the name of Jesus.

LOG-OFF: Evening Prayers

Enter and make these declarations over your life and church (pray each point at least 5 minutes; this is will give you a total of at least 60 minutes in evening prayer).

1. Under the covering of the Superior Blood of the Living Christ, I dedicate and claim, all our cities for Jesus, in Jesus' name.
2. Under the covering of the Superior Blood of the Living Christ, Let the blessings and presence of the Lord, be experienced in all our cities, in the name of Jesus.
3. Under the covering of the Superior Blood of the Living Christ, I decree, total paralysis on lawlessness, immorality and drug-addiction in this country, in the name of Jesus.

4. Under the covering of the Superior Blood of the Living Christ, Let the power, love and glory of God be established in our land, in the name of Jesus.
5. Under the covering of the Superior Blood of the Living Christ, Let there be thirst and hunger for God, in the hearts of Christians of this nation, in the name of Jesus.
6. Under the covering of the Superior Blood of the Living Christ, O Lord, deposit the spirit of revival in USA (mention your own nation too).
7. Under the covering of the Superior Blood of the Living Christ, O Lord, lay Your hands of power and might upon the Armed Forces and Police, establishments and institutions, universities and colleges of this country.
8. Under the covering of the Superior Blood of the Living Christ, Let the resurrection power, of the Lord Jesus Christ fall upon our economy, in the name of Jesus.
9. Let there be fruitfulness and prosperity in every area of this country, in the name of Jesus.
10. Under the covering of the Superior Blood of the Living Christ, I command, every threat to the political, economic and social stability in the land to be paralyzed, in the name of Jesus.
11. Under the covering of the Superior Blood of the Living Christ, I frustrate, every satanic external influence over our nation, in the name of Jesus.
12. Under the covering of the Superior Blood of the Living Christ, I command confusion and disagreement, among the heathen planning to cage the nation in evil legislations, in Jesus' name.

DAY 16

Intercessory Prayer

You'll enlist with God on behalf of the Earth to be an intercessor for Church crisis. You'll devote this whole day praying for the topic indicated in the crisis. As you intercede on behalf of the church and the world, may Heaven speedily answer your personal prayer request. May Almighty God do for you, even as you pray for the pastors of the church.

INTERCESSOR:
Time:
TOPIC: Unity Among Pastors

COVENANTED PRAYER:

> *That they all may be one; as*
> *you, Father, are in me, and I in*
> *you, that they also may be one*
> *in us: that the world may*

believe that you have sent me.
[John 17:21]

Theme: The Mission Is Not Impossible

Scripture: "But Jesus beheld *them*, and said unto them, With men this is impossible; but with God all things are possible." – Mathew 19:26

"Verily, verily, I say unto you, He that believeth on me, the works that I do shall he do also; and greater *works* than these shall he do; because I go unto my Father." – John 14:12

Problem: The church is dying because the fore-front is paralyzed and dying. The pastors are not in sync with each other and are unwilling to partner or network with each other unless it is in their self-interest. Jesus said, "If a kingdom be divided against itself, that kingdom cannot stand; if a house be divided against itself, that house cannot stand. And if Satan were to rise up against himself and be divided, he would not be able to stand, but it would be his end." In the same manner, if the pastors are divided against each other, and will not stand in unity to fellowship together, then they will fall apart. If they fall apart, the church will collapse. For the Bible says, smite the shepherd and you will scatter the flock. The church age has ended because the love among brethren has waxed cold.

Assignment: Pray that several pastors in the Bronx, from denominational lines, racial backgrounds and all tongues, will join together to lead a Christian movement. May your prayer answer show signs of pastoral unity or oneness in your local church, cities, nations and the world. As you pray, ask for signs, proofs, and tangible evidence that your prayer has be answered. Let there be a testimony.

Duration:

CHAPTER 5
WEEK III: I Mourned

And it came to pass, when I heard these words, that I ...
mourned certain days ... before the God of heaven. –
Nehemiah 1:4

5

WEEK THREE – I
Mourned

It is God's sincere desire for each of us to know Him up-
close and personally. He continually calls us to come into
His presence so that we can have sweet communion and
fellowship with Him. In that sweet communion and
fellowship, we will find and experience His faithfulness,
grace, and blessings.

We once again visit Nehemiah in his prayer closet as he cried out for God's agenda:

> *"As soon as I heard these*
> *words...I mourned many*
> *days..." (Neh. 1:4).*

We see his desperation as he yearns for God's voice in this matter. How many of us could afford to sit in God's presence until He speaks to us? Do we even have an atmosphere for His presence to manifest? But in this illustration, Nehemiah creates an atmosphere for God to manifest and reveal His agenda. In creating an atmosphere appropriate for the presence of God to manifest, Nehemiah made a deliberate effort by first sitting to meditate and restrict his daily routines, then he went into a time of travailing, indicated by his cries. Next we see him in another dimension revealed in his state of mourning.

There's a difference between weeping and mourning. Weeping may endure for a night, whilst joy comes in the morning. (Psalm 30:5). However, there are days or periods when weeping before God, doesn't provoke divine intervention and fails to yield an atmosphere of His presence. This calls to mind Elijah weeping before the LORD at the juniper tree:

> *"But he himself went a day's*
> *journey into the wilderness,*
> *and came and sat down under a*
> *juniper tree: and he requested*
> *for himself that he might die;*
> *and said, It is enough; now, O*

LORD, take away my life; for I
am not better than my fathers."
– 1 Kings 19:4.

Nevertheless, it wasn't until a month later, precisely 40 days later, that we are told that Elijah finally broke through and had an invitation to God's presence:

The LORD said, "Go out and
stand on the mountain in the
presence of the LORD, for the
LORD is about to pass by." –
1 Kings 19:11.

Such an elongated phase of weeping prayerfully before the LORD is what Nehemiah meant by, "I mourned several days." The difference between weeping and mourning is dependent on the space of time. For instance, you can weep for the loss of a loved one for a day or some days; but mourning can continue beyond days and even for years. It is common to see people who are still mourning their loved ones after several years. Nevertheless, it's rather uncommon to see Christians in a state of spiritual mourning for days, in order to invoke God's presence. What do we gain in mourning a loved one for years? How much shall we gain if we can mourn on God for years?

Nehemiah was in this agonizing state of prayer for quite some time. What instigated this protruded prayer began as follows:

"The words of Nehemiah the
son of Hachaliah. And it came

133

*to pass in the month Chisleu, in
the twentieth year, as I was in
Shushan the palace..." –
Nehemiah 1:1*

It can also be understood by reading chapter 2 that
Nehemiah prayed until the month Nisan:

*"And it came to pass in the month Nisan, in the twentieth
year of Artaxerxes the king..." – Nehemiah 2:1.*

It is imperative to note the space of time that he spent
before God in order to download the divine agenda for his
life. The month Chisleus on the Hebrew calendar is
equivalent to our calendar year November to December,
whilst the month Nisan is equivalent to March to April on
our calendar. The month Chisleus is considered the month
of dreams or revelations. It is remarkable to note that
Nehemiah began to pray during a prophetic season when
divine encounters and experiences are expected. And he
ceased prayer four months later in the month Nisan, which
is known to be the month of the Ecclesiastic. It is the
Levitical month where assignments and messages are
released.

It is proper then to conclude that by starting his prayer in
the month Chisleu, Nehemiah had expectations of
encountering God to download His divine assignment and
mandate. In reading Nehemiah chapter 2 in its entirety,
the reader will note the results of the prayer season.
Likewise, you and I have also embarked on these 40 days
of fasting so that we will encounter Him to discover and
download His agenda and assignment for our lives and

church. If weeping will not do, then we must desperately and deliberately declare a state of mourning in our prayer closets.

I remember the story I read several years ago of a pastor who ministered a century ago to a decadent community. After several attempts to reach out to the lost, the church failed to make any impact and to grow. He joined Nehemiah in a desperate state of prayer, and wrote this message in front of his church door:

"This church will either have revival or a funeral..."

Can you my friend, precious believer, get to that point in your life as a Christian, where you can say, "I will either have revival (an encounter with God) or a funeral (a state of mourning over my spiritual inadequacy)?"

Day 17

If you want deeper intimacy with God; if you want to grow in His truth and power; if you desire a Godly change in your lives, it's important for your heart to mourn out to Him. Deeper relationships require deeper commitments. Weeping may endure for a night. It is a temporal act, but if you want a long-standing, permanent relationship, then you need to enter into a state of mourning in His presence.

> *How lovely is Your tabernacle, O Lord of hosts! My soul longs, yes, even faints for the courts of the Lord; my heart and my flesh cry out for the living God. Even the sparrow has found a home, and the swallow a nest for herself, where she may lay her young—even Your altars, O Lord of hosts, my King and my God. (Psalm 84:1-3).*

The Psalmist points out that even birds recognize the sweetness of God's presence. Hence, in verse three, we see that the psalmist longs for God's presence so much that he is envious of the ability of the birds to dwell so close to the presence of the Lord. That word, "longs", is a state of elongated desire, waiting, and fervency. When tears are elongated, it enters the state of mourning. The word lovely (Strong's, 3039) in verse one can be translated "loved or beloved." The psalmist loved to dwell in God's presence so much that his whole being was mourning out for God. In the Old Testament, the presence of God dwelt in the Holy of Holies in the temple in Jerusalem, and therefore, the psalmist longs for the courts of the Lord.

A desperate state to be in God's presence is the present need of today's believers. We need believers who will either have God's presence or nothing at all. Do you feel His presence on a daily basis in your life? If our passion for His presence can match up with our actions, we will fulfill scriptures.

LOG-ON: Morning Prayers

Enter and make these declarations over your life and church (pray each point at least 5 minutes; this is will give you a total of at least 60 minutes in morning prayer).

1. Under the covering of the Superior Blood of Yeshua the Messiah, O God, let my desire for you burn and grow as wild flames.
2. Under the covering of the Superior Blood of Yeshua the Messiah, O LORD, revive me, bring back my spirit from dormancy and stir up my soul to fall in love with you once again.
3. Under the covering of the Superior Blood of Yeshua the Messiah, O LORD, create in me a clean heart, and turn my affections toward you daily.
4. Under the covering of the Superior Blood of Yeshua the Messiah, O LORD, purify my thoughts, guard my tongue, keep my ears from hearing gossips and my eyes from seeing lustful desires.
5. Under the covering of the Superior Blood of Yeshua the Messiah, O my Father, I declare with Job, that I have made a covenant with my eyes not to look upon anyone lustfully, or have an envious desire for what is not mine.
6. Under the covering of the Superior Blood of Yeshua the Messiah, O my Father, restore your right Spirit within me, and stir up my spirit to yearn for you more daily.
7. Under the covering of the Superior Blood of Yeshua the Messiah, O LORD, cause me to have faith in you, and to believe in your status.

8. Under the covering of the Superior Blood of Yeshua the Messiah, My Father and my Creator, speak to me in my dreams, and grant me visions of you daily.
9. Under the covering of the Superior Blood of Yeshua the Messiah, Oh LORD, open the eyes of my understanding, and give me revelations of You and Your Ways.
10. Under the covering of the Superior Blood of Yeshua the Messiah, Oh LORD, reveal to me all hidden mysteries concerning my life, my family, and the world.
11. Under the covering of the Superior Blood of Yeshua the Messiah, Oh LORD, teach me to love others, as You have loved me.
12. Under the covering of the Superior Blood of Yeshua the Messiah, My Father and my Creator, make me a part of your plan for my generation, and use me to fulfill Your will here on earth.

LOG-OFF: Evening Prayers

Enter and make these declarations over your life and church (pray each point at least 5 minutes; this is will give you a total of at least 60 minutes in evening prayer).

1. Under the covering of the Superior Blood of Yeshua the Messiah, O God, I thank You for You are good to me and your love endures forever, in the name of Jesus.
2. Under the covering of the Superior Blood of Yeshua the Messiah, O God, I thank You for your faithfulness and mercy over my life, in the name of Jesus.
3. Under the covering of the Superior Blood of Yeshua the Messiah, O God, I thank You for always being there for me anytime I call upon You in trouble, in the name of Jesus.
4. Under the covering of the Superior Blood of Yeshua the Messiah, O God, I thank You for not allowing the enemy to prevail over me, in the name of Jesus.
5. Under the covering of the Superior Blood of Yeshua the Messiah, O God I give You thanks for everything you have done for me and my family, in the name of Jesus.
6. Under the covering of the Superior Blood of Yeshua the Messiah, O God, I thank You, for taking Your rightful place in my life, in the name of Jesus.
7. Under the covering of the Superior Blood of Yeshua the Messiah, O God, I thank You, for You are great and worthy of praise, in the name of Jesus.

8. Under the covering of the Superior Blood of Yeshua the Messiah, O God, I thank You, for Your mercy endures forever, in the name of Jesus.

9. Under the covering of the Superior Blood of Yeshua the Messiah, O God, I thank You, for not allowing this situation to weigh me down, in the name of Jesus.

10. Under the covering of the Superior Blood of Yeshua the Messiah, O God, I thank you, because You gave me great joy and peace, in the name of Jesus.

11. Under the covering of the Superior Blood of Yeshua the Messiah, O God, I thank you, for You have delighted in me and have lifted me up above my foes, in the name of Jesus.

12. Under the covering of the Superior Blood of Yeshua the Messiah, O God, I thank You for sending Your only begotten Son to die for my sin and You declared at the cross that "it is finished".

Day 18

To appoint unto them that mourn in Zion, to give unto them beauty for ashes, the oil of joy for mourning, the garment of praise for the spirit of heaviness; that they might be called trees of righteousness, the planting of the LORD, that he might be glorified.

Praise ushers us into His Presence. To cultivate the presence of God, you must change your garment of mourning into a garment of praise.

Never miss the opportunity to praise God in hard times. You may be feeling hopeless, joyless, unfulfilled, frustrated, depressed, in debt and shattered, but if you can literally gather courage and sing and praise God, there'll be a turning around for you today.

Blessed are those who dwell in Your house; they will still be praising You.

Blessed is the man whose strength is in You, whose heart is set on pilgrimage. As they pass through the Valley of Baca, they make it a spring; the rain also covers it with pools. They go from strength to strength; each one appears before God in

Zion. (vs. 4-7).

It is important for us to always keep in mind that praise is one of the keys that opens the door into God's presence. We want our hearts to be so set on seeking God that no matter what difficulty we face we make it a place of praise. As we pass through the Valley of Baca (mourning—Strong's, 1056), we will make it a place of praise.

The Valley of Baca (Noted in vs. 6)

By translation, Baca means weeping, or a state of mourning in the Hebrew tongue. It is a place of lamentation and agonizing. When the Israelites traveled to Jerusalem to the Temple of God for worship, they had to pass through the Valley of Baca; a wilderness atmosphere saturated with a spiritual and physical state of depression and danger. It was in this place that David found himself in this Psalm. Sometimes we can all find ourselves in the Valley of Baca, where God is out of the picture. It is a place deprived of divine intervention and satisfaction. Have you ever cried, "why me LORD" or "why is this happening to me LORD" or "I am tired of this LORD"? Well if so, then you have found yourself a personal Valley of Baca. David in this state, showed us a sense of desperation for the things of God. He yearned to be in God's presence, instead of this state of self-pity and hopelessness.

The Psalmist tells us that those who lean on God can escape Baca through praising God even in their wilderness experience. This is an act of faith; that despite the circumstances, we can count it all joy when we fall in diverse trails and temptation. Our God is yet able to deliver us from all of it. We can indeed have faith and praise Him knowing that "many are the afflictions of the righteous but the LORD delivers them from all of it." You can't escape your Valley of Baca by sitting idle in defeat. You can do exactly the opposite of what the situation demands of you. Praise is a weapon against reproach and desolation. We do not praise God after He delivers us. Faith tells us to praise

Him in the sight of the problem and reporting to the problem that "we are persuaded in whom we have believed; that what we have entrusted to Him, He is faithful and able to keep it."

So Nehemiah said, "I mourned several days." Although he also found himself in his own Valley of Baca, he ceased not to cry to God night and day for 4 months, until there was a divine intervention. Don't give up, there's victory in praising God. Let this week be a week of Praises and Thanksgiving to God for you.

LOG-ON: Morning Prayers

Enter and make these declarations over your life and church (pray each point at least 5 minutes; this is will give you a total of at least 60 minutes in morning prayer).

1. Under the covering of the Superior Blood of Yeshua the Messiah, O God, I thank You for making it impossible for generational problems and curses to prosper in my life, in the name of Jesus.
2. Under the covering of the Superior Blood of Yeshua the Messiah, O Lord, I thank You for breaking the

curse of limitation and stagnation upon my life, in the name of Jesus.

3. Under the covering of the Superior Blood of Yeshua the Messiah, Father, I thank You for accepting me as one of Your children who will enter heaven despite of my sins of yesterday, in the name of Jesus.

4. Under the covering of the Superior Blood of Yeshua the Messiah, Father, I thank you, that even at the cross of Calvary, you declared to me that all my trials are over, in the name of Jesus.

5. Under the covering of the Superior Blood of Yeshua the Messiah, I thank You, for you have done great and mighty things for me, in the name of Jesus.

6. Under the covering of the Superior Blood of Yeshua the Messiah, O God, I thank you for being the strength of my soul.

7. Under the covering of the Superior Blood of Yeshua the Messiah, O God, I thank you for giving wisdom to the wise and knowledge to the discerning, in the name of Jesus.

8. Under the covering of the Superior Blood of Yeshua the Messiah, Father, I thank you for loving me with a perfect love, in the name of Jesus.

9. Under the covering of the Superior Blood of Yeshua the Messiah, Father, I worship You, for you are able to do more than we can ever ask for, in the name of Jesus.

10. Under the covering of the Superior Blood of Yeshua the Messiah, O God, I thank You, for your love is the ultimate answer to everything we face, in the name of Jesus.

11. Under the covering of the Superior Blood of Yeshua the Messiah, Father, we thank, you for you have

shown us in Jesus that everything is safe in Your hands, in the name of Jesus.

12. Under the covering of the Superior Blood of Yeshua the Messiah, I will give You thanks in the great assembly; among throngs of people I will praise You.

LOG-OFF: Evening Prayers

Enter and make these declarations over your life and church (pray each point at least 5 minutes; this is will give you a total of at least 60 minutes in evening prayer).

1. Under the covering of the Superior Blood of Yeshua the Messiah, Thank You Jesus this morning for waking me up into this new day. All glory is yours, in Jesus' name.

2. Under the covering of the Superior Blood of Yeshua the Messiah, Fill my heart O Lord, with sweet melody in honor of Your holy name.

3. Under the covering of the Superior Blood of Yeshua the Messiah, Today O Lord, forgive me of all my sins, both known and unknown in Jesus' name.

4. Under the covering of the Superior Blood of Yeshua the Messiah, My Father, if there is anything in my life that will make you not accept my fasting this day, please remove it now in Jesus' name.

5. Under the covering of the Superior Blood of Yeshua the Messiah, Lord of all ages, we thank You for

Your ageless love and Your endless patience with Your wayward children.

6. Under the covering of the Superior Blood of Yeshua the Messiah, Father, give me the grace to preoccupy myself with praising you throughout this year.

7. Under the covering of the Superior Blood of Yeshua the Messiah, Father, accept my daily sacrifice of praise this year, in the name of Jesus.

8. Under the covering of the Superior Blood of Yeshua the Messiah, O God I offer you perfect and perpetual praise this year

9. Under the covering of the Superior Blood of Yeshua the Messiah, I declare that praise will be my unfailing and life changing weapon this year in Jesus name

10. Under the covering of the Superior Blood of Yeshua the Messiah, I receive the grace to live the life of praise in Jesus name.

11. Under the covering of the Superior Blood of Yeshua the Messiah, Father give me a new beginning and make this year the best ever, in Jesus name.

12. Under the covering of the Superior Blood of Yeshua the Messiah, O Mighty God, as I lift you up, be lifted up in my life, my family and my church, in Jesus name.

DAY 19

Knowing the value of mourning before God, the Psalmist declares:

> *But as for me, when they were*
> *sick, my clothing was*
> *sackcloth: I humbled my soul*
> *with fasting; and my prayer*
> *returned into mine own bosom.*
> *I behaved myself as though he*
> *had been my friend or brother:*
> *I bowed down heavily, as one*
> *that mourneth for his mother.*
> *– Psalm 34:13-14*

What is missing in church today are believers who understand the power of mourning before God. We lack the genuine power of divinity because we lack compassion in our spirit. David the King, records how he entered a season of mourning and fasting for someone who was not a friend, or a relative, but an enemy. When he heard that his enemy was sick, he was overcome with compassion; he put on sackcloth and fasted and mourned. In fact, so intense was his mourning for this sick enemy who was near death, that David tells us he mourned as though his own mother was dead.

There are few believers in this age, who will lay aside their food for several days, to mourn for the deliverance of an enemy. These are the days when we pray for all enemies to die by fire and by thunder. David was no stranger to such judgmental prayers, but here, in this instance, he reveals that compassion triumphs over judgment. To this the apostle James later recorded, "For judgment is without mercy to one who has shown no mercy. Mercy triumphs over judgment". (James 2:13 ESV).

It is spontaneous and innate to weep and mourn if a loved one is facing death, or at the death of a loved one. However, to weep and mourn for an enemy, is the compassion of divinity.

Nehemiah's reaction to Hanani's story speaks about two Christians.

Note this:

"And it came to pass, when I heard these words, that I sat down and wept, and mourned certain days, and fasted, and prayed before the God of heaven…" (Nehemiah 1:4).

Why was Nehemiah moved by the tragedy in the city of Jerusalem, but Hanani expressed no grief? Why are we told that Nehemiah mourned several days, but Hanani seemed unaffected. What moves you to tears? What moves you to mourn? Does the state of your Christian life move you? Does your spiritual growth grieve you daily? Does the ill condition of the church today move you? Have you ever declared a whole season of mourning and fasting for your church? Have you ever declared a 40-day fasting for an adversary in your life, that God will show them mercy? At times we interact with people we don't like, but we cannot afford to spend weeks and months or even years in prayer for them. Sometimes, by the counsel of a pastor, we'll pray for such a one for a day or two and move to the conclusion that they won't change. Make a list today, of people, churches, and things that you must mourn for God's mercy.

LOG-ON: Morning Prayers

Enter and make these declarations over your life and church (pray each point at least 5 minutes; this is will give you a total of at least 60 minutes in morning prayer)

1. Under the covering of the Superior Blood of Jesus the Christ, Oh God, I release mercy upon anyone who has offended and hurt me, in Jesus name. Pray for someone you dislike or someone you upset or upsets you every time you meet them.

2. Under the covering of the Superior Blood of Jesus the Christ, My father, my Creator, let your mercy prevail over judgment over your church, in Jesus

name. Pray for your church. Seriously and sincerely, mourn on God that a change will be seen.

3. Under the covering of the Superior Blood of Jesus the Christ, I pray for peace and the wind of stability in my family in the name of Jesus. Pray for your family; mention all those you love by name, and pray for family unity, peace, prosperity, stability, and good health. Please spend considerable time.

4. Under the covering of the Superior of Blood of Jesus the Christ, I pray for my pastor to receive divine boldness, physical strength and divine power, in the name of Jesus. Pray for your pastors; many pastors are stressed, depressed, at the point of committing suicide and some are quitting the ministry.

5. Under the covering of the Superior of Blood of Jesus the Christ, I pray for wisdom, counsel, understanding and divine skill for the leadership and workers in my church, in Jesus name. Pray for the church leadership; that they may be impacted by the Spirit of God to lead with an exemplary life.

6. Under the covering of the Superior of Blood of Jesus the Christ, I pray and release this nation from any generational judgment originating from idol worship; occultic worship and satanism, in Jesus name.

7. Under the covering of the Superior of Blood of Jesus the Christ, I overrule any evil counsel permeating Congress and the White House, in Jesus name. Pray for the body responsible for legislations and decision making in the nation where you belong.

8. Under the covering of the Superior of Blood of Jesus the Christ, I declare the influence of God Almighty to arrest every decision maker in the Supreme Court and impact them with divine instructions, in Jesus name. Pray for the judicial body or judges in the nation where you belong.

9. Under the covering of the Superior of Blood of Jesus the Christ, O God intervene now in the affairs of this city and my neighborhood, in Jesus name.

10. Under the covering of the Superior of Blood of Jesus the Christ, O God, bring a change in my job place. I pray for salvation of souls at my workplace, in the name of Jesus.

11. Under the covering of the Superior of Blood of Jesus the Christ, My father and my Creator, let your presence be made known in this generation, in Jesus name.

12. Under the covering of the Superior of Blood of Jesus the Christ, O God, use me like you used Nehemiah to transform my nation, in Jesus name.

LOG-OFF: Evening Prayers

and make these declarations over your life and church (pray each point at least 5 minutes; this is will give you a total of at least 60 minutes in evening prayer)

1. Under the covering of the Superior Blood of Jesus the Christ, Father, create a thirst and hunger for God and holiness in our lives, in the name of Jesus.

2. Under the covering of the Superior Blood of Jesus the Christ, O Lord, send down the fire of revival into the body of Christ.

3. Under the covering of the Superior Blood of Jesus the Christ, O Lord, break and refill your ministers afresh.

4. Under the covering of the Superior Blood of Jesus the Christ, Let there be full and fresh outpouring of the Holy Ghost, upon the ministers of God, in the name of Jesus.

5. Under the covering of the Superior Blood of Jesus the Christ, O Lord, give unto our ministers the power for effective prayer lives.

6. Under the covering of the Superior Blood of Jesus the Christ, O Lord, release faithful, committed, dedicated and obedient labourers into the vineyard.

7. Under the covering of the Superior Blood of Jesus the Christ, By the blood of Jesus, let all sins, ungodliness, idolatry and vices cease in the land, in the name of Jesus.

8. Under the covering of the Superior Blood of Jesus the Christ, I break every evil covenant and dedication made upon our land, in the name of Jesus.

9. Under the covering of the Superior Blood of Jesus the Christ, I plead the blood of Jesus, over the nation, in Jesus' name.

10. Under the covering of the Superior Blood of Jesus the Christ, I decree the will of God for this land, whether the devil likes it or not, in the name of Jesus.

11. Under the covering of the Superior Blood of Jesus the Christ, Let all contrary powers and authorities in the USA (mention your own nation here too), be confounded and be put to shame, in the name of Jesus.

12. Under the covering of the Superior Blood of Jesus the Christ, I close every satanic gate in every city of this country, in Jesus' name.

DAY 20

The Church Needs Hired Mourners

In ancient times, people were hired to mourn and lament at funerals. Thus, the Prophet Amos says,

> *Therefore the LORD, the God*
> *of hosts, the Lord, saith thus;*
> *Wailing shall be in all streets;*
> *and they shall say in all the*
> *highways, Alas! alas! and they*
> *shall call the husbandman to*
> *mourning, and such as are*
> *skillful of lamentation to*
> *wailing. - Amos 5:16*

The world was in such a condition that the prophet Amos, called out for a national mourning. The conditions were so difficult that even the husbandman (the farmer) was called upon to take the lead in mourning. The farmer, whose vocation it was to tilt the land, plough the land, and plant seeds, was called to mourn. Why? Because this was the year when the harvest was destroyed; this was the year when the farmer could not reap what he or she had sown.

The world today is also in a national crisis. How many there are today, who are working hard but not prospering? How many there are in our churches now, who are striving to reap what they've planted but in vain? Many are frustrated because their labor has not yield any good fruit.

Here then is the trumpet call: "...call the husbandman (the farmer) to mourn." Oh that we had such amongst us today, in our church. In this fasting season, who will take up the challenge to mourn the present state of our churches, our Christianity, our nation, and our cold-love for the things of God? Let those who have lost their jobs, who have little to eat, who are sick, who are barely making a living; those who have labored but in vain, rise in our midst and take the lead to mourn for us.

The prophet here pronounces a time when the streets of the city shall be desolate, wailing shall be heard in all corners of the nation, and even strangers who pass through will stand amazed and lament the state of the nation. People will cry woe, woe, woe, for the miserable conditions and crisis in which they find themselves. These are difficult times; these are times of fear, hopelessness, dark times in the world when there's no love for God, even among the believers. The hearts of many shall wax cold, and many will fall from grace for lack of faith. We live in times, when many Christians cannot stand to be persecuted; when many cannot wait on God for five to twenty years without losing faith. We live in a fast-food, microwave generation, when our prayers must be answered as fast as we bend our knees and rise. If God does not answer us soon enough, we lose hope, quit church, abandon the faith, and live in hatred and bitterness of the things of God.

This is a call not just for those who have suffered loss, but for some amongst us whose duty it is to mourn in such crisis. We need those who are skilled of lamentation. We need to summon those whose calling it is to intercede for this crisis hour; those who have the art of mourning and are expert in making moans and using sorrowful sounds. We need intercessors such as those who were hired to assist at funerals and other doleful occasions. Will you rise to the challenge to a mournful state of prayer today?

LOG-ON: Morning Prayers

Enter and make these declarations over your life and church (pray each point at least 5 minutes; this is will give you a total of at least 60 minutes in morning prayer).

1. O Lord, restore the Later Rain Glory of your church, in the name of Jesus.
2. Under the covering of the Superior Blood of Jesus the Christ, Every Christian marriage that has been re-arranged by the enemy, be corrected in the name of Jesus. Pray for the restoration of Christian marriages. The enemy is destroying the Church by breaking up marriages.
3. Under the covering of the Superior Blood of Jesus the Christ, O Lord, let the spirit of wisdom, judgment, submission, gentleness, obedience to God's word, faithfulness in the home, come upon Christian homes, in the name of Jesus.
4. Under the covering of the Superior Blood of Jesus the Christ, O Lord, remove every wrong spirit from the midst of Your children and put in the right spirit, in the name of Jesus.
5. Under the covering of the Superior Blood of Jesus the Christ, I take authority over the plans and activities of satan on ministers' homes, in the name of Jesus.
6. Under the covering of the Superior Blood of Jesus the Christ, O Lord, increase the power and strength of the ministration of Your word amongst us, in the name of Jesus.
7. Let the kingdom of Christ come into every nation by fire, in the name of Jesus.

8. Under the covering of the Superior Blood of Jesus the Christ, O Lord, dismantle every man-made program in the body of Christ and set up Your own program, in the name of Jesus.

9. Under the covering of the Superior Blood of Jesus the Christ, I challenge and pull down the forces of disobedience in the lives of the saints, in the name of Jesus.

10. Under the covering of the Superior Blood of Jesus the Christ, I command these blessings, on the body of Christ and ministers: -love, joy, peace, longsuffering, gentleness, goodness, faith, meekness, temperance, divine healing, divine health, fruitfulness, progress, the gift of healing, prophecy, discerning of spirits, the word of wisdom, the word of knowledge, the working of miracles, diverse kinds of tongues, interpretation of tongues, beauty and glory of God, righteousness and holiness, dedication and commitment.

11. Under the covering of the Superior Blood of Jesus the Christ, Let every evil throne in this country, be dashed to pieces, in Jesus' name.

12. Under the covering of the Superior Blood of Jesus the Christ, I bind all negative forces, operating in the lives of the leaders of this country, in the name of Jesus.

LOG-OFF: Evening Prayers

Enter and make these declarations over your life and church (pray each point at least 5 minutes; this is will give you a total of at least 60minutes in evening prayer)

1. Under the covering of the Superior Blood of Jesus the Christ, O Lord, lay Your hands of fire and power upon all our leaders (in the church, the family, and the nation), in the name of Jesus.

2. Under the covering of the Superior Blood of Jesus the Christ, I bind every dark, incestuous and evil altars in this country, in Jesus' name.

3. Under the covering of the Superior Blood of Jesus the Christ, Let the Prince of Peace, reign in every department of this nation, in the name of Jesus.

4. Under the covering of the Superior Blood of Jesus the Christ, Let every anti-gospel spirit, be frustrated and be rendered impotent, in the name of Jesus.

5. Under the covering of the Superior Blood of Jesus the Christ, O Lord, give us leaders (in the family, in the church, and in the nation) who will see their roles as a calling, instead of an opportunity to amass wealth.

6. Under the covering of the Superior Blood of Jesus the Christ, Let all forms of unGodliness be destroyed, by the divine fire of burning, in the name of Jesus.

7. Under the covering of the Superior Blood of Jesus the Christ, O Lord, let our leaders (in the family, in

the church, in the nation) be filled with divine understanding and wisdom.

8. Under the covering of the Superior Blood of Jesus the Christ, O Lord, let our leaders (in the family, in the church, and in the nation) follow the counsel of God and not of man and demons.

9. Under the covering of the Superior Blood of Jesus the Christ, O Lord, let our leaders (in the family, in the church, and in the nation) have the wisdom and knowledge of God.

10. Under the covering of the Superior Blood of Jesus the Christ, O Lord, let our government be the kind that would obtain Your direction and leading.

11. Under the covering of the Superior Blood of Jesus the Christ, Let every satanic altar in this country, receive the fire of God and be burned to ashes, in the name of Jesus.

12. Under the covering of the Superior Blood of Jesus the Christ, I silence, every satanic prophet, priest and practitioner, in the mighty name of Jesus. I forbid them from interfering with the affairs of this nation, in the name of Jesus.

DAY 21

A Need for Deep Repentance

The church is in a state of pandemonium. Active sinning is the norm of the day in the believer's life. There's no more remorse for lying, gossiping, stealing, sexual immoralities, backbiting and materialism. These sins have become a lifestyle; we boldly call it, "my weakness" instead of a sin that God hates.

For this Jeremiah gave a message at the Temple Gate, condemning the false worship of the people of God. However, they continued in sin whilst having a sense of false security that the covenant of God with Abraham, Isaac and Jacob would protect them. Their refusal to repent was irrational, forgetting that God is "angry with the sinner everyday" (Psalm 7:11) and He will not fail to bring every sin to judgment. For this, God warned them through His prophet Jeremiah:

> *Thus says the Lord of hosts: Consider and call*

for the mourning
women, That they may
come; And send for
skillful wailing women,
That they may come.
Jeremiah 9:17 (NKJV)

The women who mourned were professional wailers. The Church Father Jerome wrote; "This custom continues to the present day in Judea, that women with disheveled locks and bared breasts in musical utterance invite all to weeping". The word "skillful" means wise – the mourners were meant to stimulate mourning among sympathizers; much like actors who stimulate some kind of emotional response from an audience.

The people were oblivious to their spiritual condition. Jeremiah instructs they hire professional mourners to come and weep over their sin and the impending judgment.

In the Sermon on the Mount Jesus said, "Blessed are those who mourn." (Matt. 5:4). The mourning Jesus makes reference to is the mourning over sin which produced repentance and leads to salvation. The verse continues "for they shall be comforted". The comfort is the comfort of forgiveness and salvation.

Let them make haste
And take up a wailing
for us, That our eyes
may run with tears, And
our eyelids gush with
water. Jeremiah 9:18-19
(NKJV)

Jeremiah informs the mourners to waste no time. Jeremiah invites the people to express that sorrow and grief with tears of despair.

Do you have Spiritual Understanding? People with spiritual understanding mourn over sin. Take this opportunity, to evaluate your lifestyle; take an inventory of how many people have been hurt or turned back from God because of you. For the mercy of God, can you cry out for repentance, for yourself, your family, your friends, your church and your nation?

LOG-ON: Morning Prayers

Enter and make these declarations over your life and church (pray each point at least 5 minutes; this is will give you a total of at least 60 minutes in morning prayer)

1. Under the covering of the Superior Blood of Jesus the Christ, My Father and my God, Let my prayer be set forth before thee as sweet incense, in Jesus name. (Psalm 141:2)
2. Under the covering of the Superior Blood of Jesus the Christ, We come before the throne of grace with boldness because of the shed blood of Jesus Christ and we repent of all wrong doing (sinful lusts, immorality in words, thoughts and deeds). We repent of every wrong heart positioning

(unforgiveness, bitterness, lying, stubbornness, fault finding, disobedience, pride, and anger), wrong mentalities (self-consciousness, unGodly imaginations, self-centeredness, self-righteousness), we ask You oh Lord, to purge us from every vice of the flesh. We repent from allowing the flesh to dictate to us, define our life-style and ignoring the promptings of the Spirit.

3. Under the covering of the Superior Blood of Jesus the Christ, We cast off every carnal desire that is alien to your standard. We repent of all forms of compromise; in our relationships, work place, businesses and with associates. We embrace the mind of Christ even as we destroy all carnal mindedness.

4. Under the covering of the Superior Blood of Jesus the Christ, We speak and declare righteousness, purity, holiness, accuracy over the atmosphere of our lives. We are not defined by the flesh. We are not who the flesh says we are. We are God's sons and translated from the kingdom of darkness into the kingdom of His dear son. We ask for the power and help of the Holy Spirit to enable us to walk and live in holiness, in Jesus name.

5. Under the covering of the Superior Blood of Jesus the Christ, We repent of all unfaithfulness and lack of diligence in stewarding God's resources put at our disposal to mature us and to build others. We ask for Godly accountability and wisdom in operating the wealth of the church, in Jesus' name.

6. Under the covering of the Superior Blood of Jesus the Christ, We repent and ask for forgiveness from Compromise, Immorality, Superficial Christianity,

Luke warmness, etc.; We repent from denominationalism/divisions/disunity and abandonment of the Great Commission. We ask for the power to witness and to evangelize our world in Jesus' name.

7. Under the covering of the Superior Blood of Jesus the Christ, We repent for making your power of non-effect and the intentional and unintentional exclusion of the Holy Spirit from Church activities (all the 5 offices, spiritual gifts and ministries not fully operational). We ask for fresh fire and oil to visit us again in Jesus' name.

8. Under the covering of the Superior Blood of Jesus the Christ, We repent for focusing on materialism - greed and avarice. We repent from financial recklessness; spending on materialistic things, instead of building your Kingdom. Help us to focus on heavenly things and to live for eternity in Jesus' name.

9. Under the covering of the Superior Blood of Jesus the Christ, We repent for competitions among pastors and ministers. Forgive us for comparing churches, roaming from one church to the other without commitment to your work. Forgive us for building the church according to man's pattern. We pray for restoration of the church leadership and the pattern of God for our church in Jesus' name.

10. Under the covering of the Superior Blood of Jesus the Christ, We repent from wrong doctrines; forgive us for projecting and empowering our character flaws. We repent from paucity of the Word because we are ashamed to share your Word. We repent for

praying less for the lack of Power in the Church, because of lack of faith and consecration.

11. Under the covering of the Superior Blood of Jesus the Christ, We repent for the days when our Church was not willing on the day of the Lord's Power/Battle.

12. Under the covering of the Superior Blood of Jesus the Christ, We repent and ask for your forgiveness for the lack of hunger for Wisdom of God, revelation, understanding, knowledge, insight, discernment, hearing from God. Forgive the carnality among Christian leaders. Also, forgive us all for not watching for Jesus' return nor calling for His kingdom to come.

LOG-OFF: Evening Prayers

".....If My people who
are called by My name
will humble themselves,
and pray and seek my
face, and turn from their
wicked ways, then I will
hear from heaven, and I
will forgive their sin and
heal their land...." –
2Chronicles 7:12-16

Enter and make these declarations over your life and church (pray each point at least 5 minutes; this is will give you a total of at least 60 minutes in evening prayer).

1. Under the covering of the Superior Blood of Jesus the Christ, We pray in repentance and take a bold stand against doctrinal error and deliberate departure from truth, in Jesus' name.

2. Under the covering of the Superior Blood of Jesus the Christ, We pray in repentance and take a bold stand against worldliness, "balaamism," or making merchandise out of the anointing. (Selling of ornaments for deliverance, handkerchiefs and charging of fees for prayers, prophecy, and deliverance).

3. Under the covering of the Superior Blood of Jesus the Christ, We pray in repentance and take a bold stand against spiritual blindness or ignorance of the prophetic scriptures, in Jesus' name.

4. Under the covering of the Superior Blood of Jesus the Christ, We pray for repentance and take a bold stand against selfish ambition, especially on the part of leadership in Jesus name.

5. Under the covering of the Superior Blood of Jesus the Christ, We pray for repentance and take a bold stand against idolatry in the name of Church tradition.

6. Under the covering of the Superior Blood of Jesus the Christ, We pray for repentance and take a bold stand against divisions and strife in the congregation.

7. Under the covering of the Superior Blood of Jesus the Christ, We pray for repentance and take a bold stand against misappropriation of the Lord's

resources. We declare the LORD's help and wisdom so that the church will have good and righteous stewards.

8. Under the covering of the Superior Blood of Jesus the Christ, We pray and take a bold stand against demonic oppression in the church, in Jesus' name.

9. Under the covering of the Superior Blood of Jesus the Christ, We make strong utterances for the deliverance of the saints imprisoned by false religious systems, in houses of bondage and spiritually "waterless places"; that there will be a massive exodus of these people and that they may come into the truth and the light of God's word.

10. Under the covering of the Superior Blood of Jesus the Christ, We pray that God will truly make our sanctuary a place of rest, a place of counsel and renewal for those who will temporarily terminate their trust, a place of fellowship for those who are alone, and a place of acceptance for those fleeing places of ignorance.

11. Under the covering of the Superior Blood of Jesus the Christ, We pray that God will give us understanding and revelation knowledge of His divine love for the whole Body of Christ in this new era as we desire to share the abundance of what we have received from God with the whole Body of Christ.

12. Under the covering of the Superior Blood of Jesus the Christ, We pray for the rains of revival and the wind of change upon our churches in Jesus' name.

DAY 22

Reflections On Psalm 84: You Must Be Present, To Experience "In God's Presence"

There is a difference between praying to God and experiencing God in prayer. If we know how much God loves us, we would not become discouraged in pursuit. Your own experience will convince you more than description and explanation. When you have enjoyed God and the sweetness of His love, you will find it hard to set your affections on anything else but Him.

To obtain God's presence in prayer, we must deal with our own shortcomings and hindrances. First, we must have a thirsty heart. You must learn to pray from your heart and not your head. The mind is so limited in its operation that it can only focus on one object at a time. Prayer offered from the heart cannot be interrupted by reason. Nothing can interrupt this type of prayer. When you have enjoyed God and the sweetness of His love, you will find it impossible to set your affections on anything other than

Him. There must be a hungry heart, willing to yield before it can receive. God desires to give His presence.

Your thirst and hunger for God is tested in dry seasons like the Valley of Baca.

God frequently conceals Himself for a purpose, like in Psalm 84, the Psalmist was yearning or longing for Him. For whatever reason, God conceals Himself out of His abundant goodness and faithfulness. During these seasons, you may begin to believe the way to exercise your faith is by a greater degree of affection or an exertion of strength and activity – NO dear believer, this is not the way. Some believers feel in such times that they must force their worship or prayer without sincerity. But truly I believe, it is rather a time for reflection and mourning for your Beloved. You must await the return of the Beloved with patient love, humility, peace and silent worship.

But by doing these things, you demonstrate to the Father that it is He alone and His good pleasure that you seek and not the selfish delights of your own satisfaction. Don't be impatient in your times of dryness, wait patiently for God. In doing so, your prayer life will increase and be renewed. In abandonment and contentment, learn to wait for the return of your Beloved, intermingle your waiting with sighs of love.

> "O LORD of hosts,
> blessed is the man that
> trusteth in thee." Psalm
> 84:12.

The true test of waiting is trusting; trusting that He has not forsaken you and will never leave you comfortless. God has not made us orphans; you're not the child of a fatherless God. Surely, they that seek Him, will find Him. Amen.

LOG-ON: Morning Prayers

Enter and make these declarations over your life and church (pray each point at least 5 minutes; this is will give you a total of at least 60 minutes in morning prayer).

1. **Under the covering of the Superior Blood of Jesus the Christ,** Father may my heart always be reminded that you are with me. Any troubles that arise, will not rise above me. The Lord will lift me up. Whatever trouble is raised against me; it will not conquer me. I will prevail in Jesus' name.

2. **Under the covering of the Superior Blood of Jesus the Christ,** I will live with your command, oh Lord, I refuse to be consumed by fear! Wherever I go, the Lord will go with me. May I never go where you are not, oh Lord. Lead me dear Lord. I receive strength and courage from the Lord, in Jesus' name.

3. **Under the covering of the Superior Blood of Jesus the Christ,** Father give me strength and wisdom to stand with others in their times of need. As you are selfless, may I be selfless as well. Let my eyes never turn away from those in need, in Jesus' name.

4. Under the covering of the Superior Blood of Jesus the Christ, Lord, may my abundance not be a reason to neglect others. Your joy is my strength, oh Lord! I will not dwell in grief, in Jesus' name.

5. Under the covering of the Superior Blood of Jesus the Christ, You are the strength of your people. Bless your people with peace in my city and in my nation. Bless us with peace, in Jesus' name.

6. Under the covering of the Superior Blood of Jesus the Christ, Lord, give me strength and courage. You will go with me. You will not leave nor forsake me, in Jesus' name.

7. Under the covering of the Superior Blood of Jesus the Christ, Lord give me grace to wait on you, even when reason says to do otherwise. As you have promised in your word, my strength is renewed as I wait on you.

8. Under the covering of the Superior Blood of Jesus the Christ, Whatever I had set out to do, I will not do it before waiting on you and it will be a resounding success. You will lead me to exceeding and abundant success, in Jesus' name.

9. Under the covering of the Superior Blood of Jesus the Christ, I will neither grow faint nor weary! The Lord is my strength, in Jesus' name.

10. Under the covering of the Superior Blood of Jesus the Christ, Father, I am strong in Jesus' name. My strength is found in you. I will wait on you, oh Lord. Even when it hurts!

11. Under the covering of the Superior Blood of Jesus the Christ, Father, I am faint, give me power. I have no might, give me strength in Jesus' name.

12. Under the covering of the Superior Blood of Jesus the Christ, Lift me, when I feel I cannot carry on. My strength is renewed. I will soar higher than I have yet soared, in Jesus' name.

LOG-OFF: Evening Prayers

Enter and make these declarations over your life and church (pray each point at least 5 minutes; this is will give you a total of at least 60 minutes in evening prayer).

1. Under the covering of the Superior Blood of Jesus the Christ, My Father and my God, Let my prayer be set forth before thee as sweet incense, in Jesus' name.
2. Under the covering of the Superior Blood of Jesus the Christ, Oh God arise and anoint me with the Gift of Discerning of Spirits.
3. Under the covering of the Superior Blood of Jesus the Christ, Oh God arise and anoint me with the Gift of Speaking in Tongues, in Jesus' name.
4. Under the covering of the Superior Blood of Jesus the Christ, Oh God arise and anoint me with the Gift of the Interpretation of Tongues in Jesus' name.

5. Under the covering of the Superior Blood of Jesus the Christ, Oh God arise and anoint me with the Gift of Healing, in Jesus' name.
6. Under the covering of the Superior Blood of Jesus the Christ, Oh God arise and anoint me with the Gift of Prophecy, in Jesus' name.
7. Under the covering of the Superior Blood of Jesus the Christ, Oh God arise and anoint me the Gift of Dream and Vision Interpretation, in Jesus name.
8. Under the covering of the Superior Blood of Jesus the Christ, Oh God arise and fill me with your Apostolic anointing in Jesus' name.
9. Under the covering of the Superior Blood of Jesus the Christ, Holy Ghost arise and fill me with your Prophetic anointing in Jesus' name.
10. Under the covering of the Superior Blood of Jesus the Christ, Holy Ghost arise fill me with your Evangelist anointing in Jesus' name.
11. Under the covering of the Superior Blood of Jesus the Christ, Holy Ghost arise fill me with your Pastoral anointing in Jesus name.
12. Under the covering of the Superior Blood of Jesus the Christ, Holy Ghost arise and fill me with your Teaching anointing in Jesus' name.

DAY 23

Reflections On Psalm 84: For A Hungry Soul, Every Bitter Thing Is Sweet

This is indeed a bitter and a sweet psalm. It tells about suffering and yet there's hope within suffering for those who seek it. I find the place of mourning before God not necessarily sweet, but a bitter ordeal to go through a process of this nature.

Nevertheless, be patient during suffering. Don't withdraw from one season to another – give yourselves totally. You will not find consolation in anything other than the love of His presence and total abandonment to it. If you will not savor His presence, you cannot savor the things of God (Matt 16:33. Prov 27:7) – for a hungry soul every bitter thing is sweet.

You end up hungering for God in the same proportion as your soul is hungering for His presence. God gives us the presence, and the presence gives us God. As soon as anything is presented to you in the form of suffering and you begin to feel resistance in your spirit, resign yourself immediately to God. Give yourself and your circumstances to Him. Then when the presence of God arrives, it will not be so burdensome because you're already in a position for it. Wait for God to reveal truth to you.

Allow Him to animate us with life. Abandonment is the means God uses to reveal His mysteries to us. Seasons of mourning are akin to seasons of abandonment and reproach, rejection and deprivation. As you feel abandoned you have no choice but to reach after Him, dwell in Him, and sink into nothingness before Him – God may take some of you aside for years at a time to reveal the enjoyment of one single mystery. If we're locked into His presence, He will reveal His secretes and mysteries to us.

Walk then in the light He has given you. If God chooses to withdraw this illumination from you – be just as willing to yield it back to Him.

Some feel incapable at first of meditating on the mysteries God reveals to you in His Word. But don't be afraid to enter into all God has for you.

God takes us through such seasons to fall in love with us. One thing I know for sure, if you love someone you only want what is best for that someone. Love is manifested in your life as a result of your closeness to God, for He is all love. Do you want to know how to love more? Then, draw closer to Him. When God comes to live in us, He brings all of His virtues. If divine love glows within you, you will not try to flee suffering and adversity. You will think of only how to please your Beloved in that circumstance. Forget yourself and your own personal ambitions. Let your love for God increase – in doing so you will learn to love the Creator more than the created.

LOG-ON: Morning Prayers

Enter and make these declarations over your life and church (pray each point at least 5 minutes; this is will give you a total of at least 60 minutes in morning prayer).

1. Under the covering of the Superior Blood of Jesus the Christ, My Father and my God, Let my prayer be set forth before thee as a sweet incense, in Jesus name. (Psalm 141:2).

2. Under the covering of the Superior Blood of Jesus the Christ, My Father and my God, please forgive me of any known and unknown sins that I and my forefathers have sinned against you and men, in Jesus name.

3. Under the covering of the Superior Blood of Jesus the Christ, Blood of Jesus, wash me from all my sins in Jesus' name.

4. Under the covering of the Superior Blood of Jesus the Christ, My Father and my God, I thank you for loving me and my loved ones, in Jesus name.

5. Under the covering of the Superior Blood of Jesus the Christ, O God arise and guide me along the best pathway for my life, in Jesus' name. (Psalm 32:8).

6. Under the covering of the Superior Blood of Jesus the Christ, O God arise and advise me, in Jesus' name. (Psalm 32:8).

7. Under the covering of the Superior Blood of Jesus the Christ, O God arise and watch over me, in Jesus' name. (Psalm 32:8).

8. Under the covering of the Superior Blood of Jesus the Christ, Teach me how to live, O Lord in Jesus' name. (Psalm 27:11).

9. Under the covering of the Superior Blood of Jesus the Christ, Lead me along the path of honesty in Jesus' name. (Psalm 27:11).
10. Under the covering of the Superior Blood of Jesus the Christ, O God arise and Show me the path you have chosen for me, in Jesus' name. (Psalm 25:12).
11. Under the covering of the Superior Blood of Jesus the Christ, Show me thy ways, O LORD in Jesus' name. (Psalm 25:4).
12. Under the covering of the Superior Blood of Jesus the Christ, Teach me thy paths O LORD in Jesus' name. (Psalm 25:4).

LOG-OFF: Evening Prayers

Enter and make these declarations over your life and church (pray each point at least 5 minutes; this is will give you a total of at least 60 minutes in evening prayer).

1. Under the covering of the Superior Blood of Jesus the Christ, My Father and my God, Let my prayer be set forth before thee as incense, in Jesus' name.
2. Under the covering of the Superior Blood of Jesus the Christ, O God arise and do a new thing in my life, in Jesus' name.
3. Under the covering of the Superior Blood of Jesus the Christ, O God arise and let new things spring forth in my life, in Jesus' name.
4. Under the covering of the Superior Blood of Jesus the Christ, O God arise and make a way in the wilderness for me, in Jesus' name.

5. Under the covering of the Superior Blood of Jesus the Christ, O God arise and make rivers in the desert for me, in Jesus' name.

6. Under the covering of the Superior Blood of Jesus the Christ, My Father and my God, turn my wailing into dancing, in Jesus' name.

7. Under the covering of the Superior Blood of Jesus the Christ, Take away my clothes of mourning, in Jesus' name.

8. Under the covering of the Superior Blood of Jesus the Christ, Clothe me with joy, in Jesus' name.

9. Under the covering of the Superior Blood of Jesus the Christ, O Lord keep my lamp burning, in Jesus' name.

10. Under the covering of the Superior Blood of Jesus the Christ, O God arise and turn my darkness into light, in Jesus' name.

11. Under the covering of the Superior Blood of Jesus the Christ, O LORD, be my shield, in Jesus' name.

12. Under the covering of the Superior Blood of Jesus the Christ, Glory of God, overshadow me, in Jesus' name.

DAY 24

Intercessory Prayer

You'll enlist with God on behalf of the Earth to be an intercessor for Church crisis. You'll devote this whole day praying for the topic indicated in the crisis. As you intercede on behalf humanity, may Heaven speedily answer your personal prayer request. May Almighty God do for you, even as you pray for others. As a point of contact, you may mention the names of people you know, to specifically pray for healing and deliverance.

INTERCESSOR:

TIME:

Theme: The Mission Is Not Impossible

Scripture: "But Jesus beheld them, and said unto them, With men this is impossible; but with God

all things are possible." – Mathew 19:26.

"Verily, verily, I say unto you, He that believeth on me, the works that I do shall he do also; and greater works than these shall he do; because I go unto my Father." – John 14:12.

Problem: There is a rise in cancer across the world, the nation, city and the Bronx. This is a universal problem, far exceeding our imagination. Cancer is turning to be a pandemic, and it is common to hear of someone, irrespective of age, having being diagnosed with this disease. In 2018, it was recorded that an estimated 1,735,350 new cases of cancer would be diagnosed in the United States and 609,640 people would die from the disease.

Cancer is the second most common cause of death in the US, exceeded only by heart disease, accounting for nearly 1 of every 4 deaths.

Assignment: This is an important assignment that will change the scope of humanity for several generations to come. The mission here is great, but it is not impossible with God. Pray that God will intervene in this diabolical sudden death and destruction of life. Pray for miraculous cures, pray for breakthrough solutions, pray for God to use someone to find a cure immediately. Time isn't on our side, in just one day, 1,700 people in the USA are killed of this demonic cancerous growth; the world depends and needs this prayer. May God grace you to avail much. As you pray may there be tangible signs of answered prayers and a testimony of the Divine hand of God in operation. Let there by new and speedy innovations in the medical field. May God grant unparalleled knowledge and understanding for those invested in cancer research.

Duration:

CHAPTER 6

WEEK IV: I FASTED

And it came to pass, when I heard these words, that I ... fasted ...
before the God of heaven.
– Nehemiah 1:4

6

WEEK FOUR: I FASTED

At this stage, you've completed 24 days of fasting; and the end of this section will mark 32 days of fasting and prayer. What're your successes so far? What're your challenges? Do you have a testimony? Have you received any revelations or visions? Whatever your experience may be at this stage, share it with your church or pastor if you're fasting with a Church. If you're fasting on your own, share it with a mature believer, your spiritual father (or mother) or your pastor.

This next stage is familiar grounds. Before we continue, lets take notes from what Nehemiah did:

> *"And it came to pass,*
> *when I heard these*
> *words, that I*
> *...fasted...before the*
> *God of heaven..."* –
> Nehemiah 1:4

The fourth thing Nehemiah did in this process was fasting.

Now, that certainly includes choices to restrict one's diet for the purpose of paying attention to God. It is noteworthy that in the ancient world meals were not like ours. We can have a sandwich with us or quickly grab something to eat and be talking on the phone and typing while we eat it, so that the experience of eating happens almost without our knowing it. In the ancient world meals were communal events. The whole family would be together. It took a long time to prepare. It was expected that you would enter into extended conversation and be part of the social network. So fasting was a deliberate attempt not only to keep from eating but to withdraw from the whole network, to stop listening to all the voices, to refrain from attending to all the responsibilities. Fasting was stepping away from the world and all its entanglements in order to spend time with God.

If that was the way it was in the ancient world, think of how much more difficult it is in the modern world to make time for God. Think of how many ways we can be contacted, and demands can be made on us for response: meetings, phones, Facebook, Instagram, snapchat, mail, e-mail, reality shows and unnecessary demands for television, and recreational activities.

It was more than just not eating food. Nehemiah was saying, "I'm stepping back. God will have space in my life; no intruders are allowed."

Maybe, you're thinking Nehemiah had nothing important to do, or that there was no risk for him. For this he responded, "for this I was sore afraid" (Nehemiah 2:2c), the reason, he says, "For I was the king's cupbearer." (Nehemiah 1:11b).

The cupbearer of the king fasted! The most important person in the king's court, who holds the life of the king in his hands, spent three to four months fasting. The cupbearer is responsible for what the king eats; unless he has inspected and tasted the food, the king will not eat. So how did Nehemiah manage to skip meals, whilst yet making sure the king was safely eating? If Nehemiah, could spare time out of his busy schedule despite the life-threatening risk, then you and I have no excuse.

JESUS FASTED

And Jesus being full of
the Holy Ghost returned
from Jordan, and was
led by the Spirit into the
wilderness, Being forty
days tempted of the
devil. And in those days
he did eat nothing: and
when they were ended,
he afterward hungered.
– Luke 4:1-2

Immediately after being baptized in the Jordan by John the Baptist, Jesus was led by the Holy Spirit to spend forty days fasting in the wilderness, Luke 4:1-2. During this forty-day period Jesus came into direct spiritual conflict with Satan. Is it possible that Satan knew from history that fasting releases God's power and that Jesus was now preparing for the ultimate decisive battle? Satan certainly did his utmost to thwart Jesus' plans at this point.

The text is revealing. In Luke 4.1, it says "And Jesus, **full of the Holy Spirit ....**" but afterwards, in Luke 4.14 we read: "And Jesus returned **in the power of the Spirit.**"

It seems that the potential of the Holy Spirit's power, which Jesus received at the time of His baptism in Jordan, only came into its full manifestation after He had completed His fast. Fasting was the final phase of preparation through which He had to pass, before entering into His public ministry.

It is one thing to be full of the Holy Spirit and another thing altogether to be "in the power of the Spirit". The former is a gift given at the initial stage of salvation, but the later is dependent on our tenacity in fasting and prayer.

Fasting in the wilderness obviously took Jesus to another level of effectiveness.

Jesus made an interesting comment in Mark 9:29. Remarking on the inability of the disciples to cast out a spirit from a boy, he says that 'this kind only comes out by prayer and fasting.' This means that some special situations that are being troubled by satanic powers are better handled by adding fasting to prayer. Again, fasting releases God's power.

DAY 25

In Luke 4 we have the record of the beginning of the Lord's Ministry. It is no surprise that it would begin with a battle with His arch-enemy, the devil. As a Spirit Filled man He is compelled into the devil's battle-ground where the long awaited [Genesis 3:15] conflict of foes would begin.

Each of us will enter a battle with the devil before we can occupy prophetic destiny. There's no victory, without a battle. To achieve greatness, you will need to contend for it. We will be tempted. The enemy will make us an offer to turn down our God-given destiny. Our first parents Adam and Eve, and our savior Jesus faced the enemy in a battle for humanity. Likewise, there's someone waiting on you to succeed in this conflict of destiny. For the sake of that one person, don't give up.

The Reasons For the Temptations

[Ref: Gen.3:15; Heb.2:14,15; 4:25; Isa.14:12-14]

1. Satan will tempt you but he will not be victorious if you're willing to pray.

2. The devil comes to tempt you because of your destiny.

3. Every war has the potential and intent to destroy destinies, recover resources and to imperialize.

4. But you shall not be a candidate of satanic conquest and assault, in Jesus' name.

5. Satan is after your destiny, and nothing more – If you're within your wilderness experience facing satanic invasion, may you pray now for your liberation.

LOG-ON: MORNING PRAYERS

Enter and make these declarations over your life and church (pray each point at least 5 minutes; this is will give you a total of at least 60 minutes in morning prayer).

1. Under the covering of the Superior Blood of Jesus the Christ, I come against any satanic vehicles of temptation, I command it to be interrupted and intercepted by the fire of the Holy Ghost.

2. Under the covering of the Superior Blood of Jesus the Christ, I overpower any demonic organized battle in my life right now and I command it to ceased by the power of the Holy Spirit, and the saving blood of Jesus Christ.

3. Under the covering of the Superior Blood of Jesus the Christ, I overrule any demonic organizers, and agents of destruction and frustration, sent into my life, I destroy their wiles and plots, in Jesus' name.

4. Under the covering of the Superior Blood of Jesus the Christ, I cancel any diabolical delay tactics and occult manipulation to destroy my destiny in the wilderness, and I command it be thwarted and overthrown by the power of Holy Ghost, in Jesus' name.

5. Under the covering of the Superior Blood of Jesus the Christ, I break any occult remote controllers and enchantments programed against my destiny, and I cast them into the consuming fire now, in Jesus' name.

6. Under the covering of the Superior Blood of Jesus the Christ, I confess and receive cleansing for any iniquities and transgressions connected to me, in Jesus' name.

7. Under the covering of the Superior Blood of Jesus the Christ, I employ the efficacy of the Superior Blood of the Living Christ to wash me from any sins that are choking my life path, in Jesus' name.

8. Under the covering of the Superior Blood of Jesus the Christ, I overrule any power (spiritual or physical) crying for my persecution, in Jesus' name.

9. Under the covering of the Superior Blood of Jesus the Christ, I silence every voice of the accuser (satan) against my life now, in Jesus' name.

10. Under the covering of the Superior Blood of Jesus the Christ, of whom I am, and whom I belong, I condemn and eject out of my body, soul, and spirit, any venom of Satan and his cohorts now, in Jesus' name. (3x)

11. Under the covering of the Superior Blood of Jesus the Christ, I boldly confess and declare that neither death nor life, neither angels nor demons, neither the present nor the future, nor any powers under and above the heavens shall be able to separate me from the covenanted love of Christ Jesus.

12. Under the covering of the Superior Blood of Jesus the Christ, O Lord of my Salvation, surround me now with the gates of praise, and cover me with the canopy of favor this year, in Jesus' name. (3x)

LOG-OFF: EVENING PRAYERS

Enter and make these declarations over your life and church (pray each point at least 5 minutes; this is will give you a total of at least 60 minutes in evening prayer).

1. Under the covering of the Superior Blood of Jesus the Christ, The Bible says because I believe and receive Jesus Christ, power has been given to me to become a son of God, and I am empowered to trample upon serpents and scorpions and all the powers of the enemy.

2. Under the covering of the Superior Blood of Jesus the Christ, I am empowered to use the name of Jesus to cast out demons and heal the sick.

3. Under the covering of the Superior Blood of Jesus the Christ, I am empowered to bind, to loose and to decree things and the Bible says wherever my voice is heard no one can ask me why.

4. Under the covering of the Superior Blood of Jesus the Christ, I do these things for my voice is the voice of a King who is full of authority.

5. Under the covering of the Superior Blood of Jesus the Christ, I am commanded and empowered by my God to subdue and to exercise dominion. For I am made a little lower than the angels and God has crowned me with glory and honor and has also made me to have dominion over all the works of His hands.

6. Under the covering of the Superior Blood of Jesus the Christ, the devil that was against my authority as a God's representative on earth has been

destroyed by Christ and once again, the keys of the kingdom of heaven are given to me and because I am a member of the body of Christ, which is the Church, the gates of hell cannot prevail against me.

7.   Under the covering of the Superior Blood of Jesus the Christ, Because the grace of God is upon my life as the light of His glory, I am full of divine favor; I am a partaker of all of heaven's spiritual blessings.

8.   Under the covering of the Superior Blood of Jesus the Christ, I am an overcomer. The Bible says whosoever is born of God overcomes the world, and this is the victory that overcomes the world, even my faith.

9.   Under the covering of the Superior Blood of Jesus the Christ, In faith I overcome unGodly worry, anxiety, heaviness of spirit, sorrow, depression, lust of the eyes and lust of the flesh.

10. Under the covering of the Superior Blood of Jesus the Christ, In faith I have overcome all the tricks of the devil, for it is written, greater is Jesus Christ that dwells in me than the devil that is in the world.

11. Under the covering of the Superior Blood of Jesus the Christ, No weapon that is formed against me shall prosper, in Jesus' name.

12. Under the covering of the Superior Blood of Jesus the Christ, In righteousness I am established; I am far from oppression, for I shall not fear any terror, for it shall not come near me.

DAY 26

Satan attempts to break Jesus' power.
[Genesis 3:15].

During the fast, Satan will attempt to diminish the power of God in your life. He'll endeavor to place you in doubt; you may sometimes question God's power, His abilities, and even His very existence. The enemy will tempt us by offering us less than we asked from God; only that he will deliver it on time. When God told Moses to tell Pharaoh to let Israel go, the enemy made an offer: "All right, go ahead," Pharaoh replied. "I will let you go into the wilderness to offer sacrifices to the LORD your God. But don't go too far away" (Exodus 8:28). Beware, the enemy has a way to make you settle for less than God wants to give you.

Take Note:

1. Satan tempted Jesus to disqualify Him [Hebrews 4:15 ...without sin...]

2. The devil will enter your life to disqualify you from what God has qualified you for.

3. He also attempted Jesus to dominate Him [Isaiah 14:12-14]

4. Satan wants control over your life: He doesn't want you to pray, read the Word, and fellowship in Church. You must deprogram his agenda if you feel his control in these areas.

5. Satanic domination is when your lifestyle is soulish and unspiritual. You desire satisfaction and self-gratification rather than to surrender to Christ.

LOG-ON: MORNING PRAYERS

Enter and make these declarations over your life and church (pray each point at least 5 minutes; this is will give you a total of at least 60 minutes in morning prayer).

1. Under the covering of the Superior Blood of Jesus the Christ, I pray and break every spirit of satanic sabotage to disqualify me, my family and my church from our divine appointment.

2. Under the covering of the Superior Blood of Jesus the Christ, I pray with urgency to terminate any demonic domination over my life, my family and my local church, in Jesus' name.

3. Under the covering of the Superior Blood of Jesus the Christ, I pray to deprogram any occult methodism to frustrate my spiritual life, my family and my church, in Jesus' name.

4. Under the covering of the Superior Blood of Jesus the Christ, I pray and ask God to cover me, my family, my church with a hostile angelic unit against any satanic attempts to make us powerless Christians.

5. Under the covering of the Superior Blood of Jesus the Christ, I pray for divine strength, enablement and empowerment for my life, my family and my church, in Jesus' name.

6. Under the covering of the Superior Blood of Jesus the Christ, The Lord shall cover me, my family, and my church with His feathers, because I have made Him my dwelling place.

7. Under the covering of the Superior Blood of Jesus the Christ, Evil shall not befall me; I shall tread upon the lion and the cobra and surely the Lord will always deliver my life, my family, and my church from the snare of the fowlers. God has made my life, my family and my church family a beneficiary of divine health through the stripes that were laid on Jesus Christ.

8. Under the covering of the Superior Blood of Jesus the Christ, Through Jesus Christ I and my family, and my church have access to the throne grace of God, to find peace with God.

9. Under the covering of the Superior Blood of Jesus the Christ, I, my family and my church have prosperity, for God will no longer withhold any good thing from us, in Jesus' name.

10. Under the covering of the Superior Blood of Jesus the Christ, I have spoken with the tongue of the learned and as it is written, I shall be justified by the words of my mouth, in Jesus' name.

11. Under the covering of the Superior Blood of Jesus the Christ, I ask that the word of God I have confessed, begin to transform my life, my family and my church to the original image God designed us to be in His book.

12. Under the covering of the Superior Blood of Jesus the Christ, I ask that the blood of Jesus wipe away every mark of reproach whether physical or spiritual.

LOG-OFF: EVENING PRAYERS

Enter and make these declarations over your life and church (pray each point at least 5 minutes; this is will give you a total of at least 60 minutes in evening prayer).

1. Under the covering of the Superior Blood of Jesus the Christ, Thank you Lord for calling me to a deeper commitment to you and making me conscious of the need to commit myself and mine to you.

2. Under the covering of the Superior Blood of Jesus the Christ, I hereby confess that I am leaving all and everything to follow you for nothing is as important to me as you.

3. Under the covering of the Superior Blood of Jesus the Christ, I have faith in you and so without any hesitation I have turned everything about my life over to you for you know better.

4. Under the covering of the Superior Blood of Jesus the Christ, I am yielded and surrendered to you and your will.

5. Under the covering of the Superior Blood of Jesus the Christ, I present myself as an obedient person to whom doing your will is an all-consuming passion. I know I am not my own anymore for I am bought with a price.

6. Under the covering of the Superior Blood of Jesus the Christ, I am separated from the world and its lusts of the flesh, of the eyes and the pride of life. I am committed to studying the word of God like never before.

7. Under the covering of the Superior Blood of Jesus the Christ, I am committing large portions of the word to memory, that I may use it both as a shield of faith and the sword of the spirit.

8. Under the covering of the Superior Blood of Jesus the Christ, I am committed to enforcing the victory of Jesus on earth and in every place I go. I am committed to a life of excellence and high standards.

9. Under the covering of the Superior Blood of Jesus the Christ, I am committed to winning souls. I am a fisher of men. I will henceforth be committed to attend prayer meetings of the church. I hereby make a new and resolute commitment to giving generously to the Lord, His course, and to the Storehouse from which I feed spiritually.
   I make this commitment from which I will not slack again.

10. Under the covering of the Superior Blood of Jesus the Christ, I am unreservedly committed to my local church, the services, vision, purpose and plans. For me, there is no such thing as partial commitment again.

11. Under the covering of the Superior Blood of Jesus the Christ, My commitment is final and I have stopped making excuses and this is deciding and defining my future for the better.

12. Under the covering of the Superior Blood of Jesus the Christ, I commit myself to the Lord as my refuge during times of hardship.

DAY 27

The Regions of Temptations In Fasting
[Luke 4:3-12; 1 John 2:15,16]

How will the devil tempt you? With what, where, when and why will he do it?

Take Note:

1. Appetites – The Lust of the Flesh [Luke 4:3,4]

    ➤ Adam & Eve gave up their rights and destiny because of an appetizing fruit.

    ➤ Esau sold his birth right to Jacob because of a bowl of stew.

    ➤ Jesus was asked by the devil to trade His destiny for a loaf of bread.

    ➤ What is the devil asking you to trade with your destiny?

➤ Has he used the desires of the flesh to entice you lately into compromising your spiritual life?

➤ Has Satan fed you something you lust after only to rob you of your divine liberty?

2. Avarice – The Lust of the Eyes [Luke 4:5-8]

➤ We walk by faith and not by sight

➤ Don't lust after what you see, but after what God has promised you.

➤ Sarah lusted after what others had, and not what God has promised them.

➤ Hannah was barren for over 20 years because she lusted after what Peninnah had, and not what God wanted to give her. Don't spend time praying for what someone has, but pray for what God wants to give you. Don't pray because of Peninnah, but pray because you know God loves you and desires to give you the best.

➤ When Hannah discovered what God had for her, she forgot about Peninnah and prayed unto God not because her adversary provoked her, but because she received divine revelation to discover what God had planned for her. The day Hannah kept her eyes off her adversary, and placed her motive on God, she went home with an answered prayer. Don't allow the enemy to busy you with so much unnecessary prayers that, you can't focus on God.

➤ Don't allow the spirit of avarice to rule over you this season. It's not every battle you must fight. Some battles are won by walking away.

➤ Don't ask because you've seen someone with it, but only ask because God has promised to give it to you.

3. Ambition – The Pride of Life [Luke 4:9-12]

➤ Satan offered Jesus the kingdoms of the world if He would bow to Him.

➤ Many have bowed to Satan only to be successful. They couldn't wait for God's way, so they took a shortcut.

➤ Many have dishonored God and worshipped Satan by using dubious means to gain wealth and fame.

➤ Satan told Jesus, if only you will worship me, "I will give you..." If you have obtained anything by means of satanic manipulations, then I plead with you settle it with God in prayer right now.

➤ Your destiny is too great to bargain with Satan for the crumbs.

➤ Moses refused to be called the son of Pharaoh's daughter or the Prince of Egypt, choosing rather to suffer affliction with the people of God, than to enjoy the pleasures of sin for a season. [Hebrews 11:24-25].

➤ Wait patiently for God's day of promotion for your life. Don't be in a haste to be successful.

LOG-ON: MORNING PRAYERS

Enter and make these declarations over your life and church (pray each point at least 5 minutes; this is will give you a total of at least 60 minutes in morning prayer).

1. Under the covering of the Superior Blood of Jesus the Christ, I pray against any unholy appetite to draw me away from the things of God.

2. Under the covering of the Superior Blood of Jesus the Christ, I pray that any enticement of satan to cause me to forfeit my God-given destiny and right, be disappointed now in Jesus' name.

3. Under the covering of the Superior Blood of Jesus the Christ, I pray that any operation of darkness to cause me to exchange my destiny for a loaf of bread or a bowl of stew, be aborted by the consuming fire of God in Jesus' name.

4. Under the covering of the Superior Blood of Jesus the Christ, I pray that any diabolical dream that involves any transaction of my destiny and liberty be annulled now by the consuming fire of God, in Jesus' name.

5. Under the covering of the Superior Blood of Jesus the Christ, I pray that any desires of the flesh, the lust of the eyes, sexual immoralities and unholy agendas used by satanic covens to ensnare my destiny must perish now by the consuming fire of God, in Jesus' name.

6. Under the covering of the Superior Blood of Jesus the Christ, I pray that I am delivered from all

covenants and parts made with known and unknown spirits knowingly or unknowingly, by the consuming fire of God, in Jesus name.

7. Under the covering of the Superior Blood of Jesus the Christ, I pray that the Holy Spirit will enable me to walk by faith and never by sight, in Jesus' name.

8. Under the covering of the Superior Blood of Jesus the Christ, I pray that the Holy Spirit will enable me not to lust after what I see but after those things that God has promised me, in Jesus' name.

9. Under the covering of the Superior Blood of Jesus the Christ, I pray I will not lust after what others have, but only after that which God has given me, in Jesus' name.

10. Under the covering of the Superior Blood of Jesus the Christ, I pray against the relentless spirit of avarice and that it be evicted from my life right now, in Jesus' name.

11. Under the covering of the Superior Blood of Jesus the Christ, I pray that my eyes will be anointed to behold the wondrous things of the LORD.

12. Under the covering of the Superior Blood of Jesus the Christ, I pray that anything satan offered to me in dreams, visions, trances, or natural occurrences be dissolved now, in the Blood of Jesus Christ.

LOG-OFF: EVENING PRAYER

Enter and make these declarations over your life and church (pray each point at least 5 minutes; this is will give you a total of at least 60 minutes in evening prayer).

1. Under the covering of the Superior Blood of Jesus the Christ, I pray that any satanic deposits or contributions into my finances, unknowingly or knowingly be eradicated by the Blood of Jesus Christ.

2. Under the covering of the Superior Blood of Jesus the Christ, I pray that any diabolic hands that lent to me or I borrowed from, perish now by the consuming fire of God, in Jesus' name.

3. Under the covering of the Superior Blood of Jesus the Christ, I pray that any false worship arising from the canals of the throne of satan be interrupted now, by the saving Blood of Jesus.

4. Under the covering of the Superior Blood of Jesus the Christ, I pray that anything I received to get ahead in life, or better my living without divine influence and outside of God's calendar for my life be forfeited now, by the consuming fire of God.

5. Under the covering of the Superior Blood of Jesus the Christ, I pray and declare the Lord will uphold me in spirit and truth.

6. Under the covering of the Superior Blood of Jesus the Christ, I pray and declare everything I lay my hands on will result in prosperity.

7. Under the covering of the Superior Blood of Jesus the Christ, I pray and declare I am committed to sowing seeds without considering the adverse circumstance of my environment.

8. Under the covering of the Superior Blood of Jesus the Christ, I pray and declare, Oh LORD, I no longer protest your call to me for a higher and total commitment.

9. Under the covering of the Superior Blood of Jesus the Christ, I pray and declare, I commit my ways to the Lord and trust in Him and He directs my paths.

10. Under the covering of the Superior Blood of Jesus the Christ, I boldly confess and declare that this year shall be my year of divine encounter and spiritual growth.

11. Under the covering of the Superior Blood of Jesus the Christ, I pray and declare that my ambition this year shall be God-filled, God-centered, and God-directed, in Jesus' name.

12. Under the covering of the Superior Blood of Jesus the Christ, I pray and declare, I will promote the work of God through my local church; I will humble myself and serve to the glory of God.

DAY 28

The Rationale Of Temptations In Fasting
[Luke 4:3-12]

Many of us fall into temptation because the devil inculcates us into justifying the sin as long as it brings income.

Take Note:

1. The end justifies the means. [Luke 4:3,4].

    - ➤ Driving a Beer Truck is alright, you have to feed your family.
    - ➤ You will fail in your spiritual walk if you fall prey to such excuses.
    - ➤ Don't agree to any unrighteous shortcuts in life if it is contrary to the Word of God.
    - ➤ It doesn't matter if you have to do it to save a life, if it is contrary to God's Word, avoid it.

God can rescue the Ark of the Covenant without Uzzah's help. (2 Sa. 6:12-19).

2. You will be better off if you serve the devil and not the Lord. [Luke 4:5-8].

   ➤ It is more profitable to gain the world than to worry about serving the Lord – "false."
   ➤ Don't do it because others are doing it and nothing bad is happening to them.
   ➤ You are a child of Destiny; a Christian by distinction, so do not do it because everyone is doing it.
   ➤ The devil will win the battle over your soul if you allow yourself to faint in serving God and slack in church going.
   ➤ Satan wants to rob you of your faithfulness to God. Be consistent and serve the LORD with all your might.

3. You can jump and God will catch you. [Luke 4:9-12].

   ➤ As Rev. Dr. Eric Achaab once said, "God will save you but not from your own carelessness." In other words, don't do it if you know it's wrong, just because you know God is merciful.
   ➤ Do not tempt God; if it is not right don't do it. Refrain from all "appearances" of sin. (1

Thess. 5:22). If, it "looks" sinful or evil, avoid it at all cost. Don't ask questions or ponder upon why you should or shouldn't.

➤ "Go ahead and charge it, the Lord will provide the money later." Have you ever heard that voice? Don't fall to this trick by the devil. Your temptation may not be on the mountain like Jesus, but yours may be a plastic card in your hand waiting to be charged. If you can't afford it, don't buy it. If you are believing for divine provision, wait for it before you act.

➤ The Law of Gravity operates irrespective of your belief system. Law states, if you jump you'll fall. Praying in tongues or wailing all night to God won't change that. Only trust and obey, there's no other way to be happy in Jesus.

➤ Seek divine wisdom toward any act of Faith.

LOG-ON: MORNING PRAYER

Enter and make these declarations over your life and church (pray each point at least 5 minutes; this is will give you a total of at least 60 minutes in morning prayer).

1. Under the covering of the Superior Blood of Jesus the Christ, I pray that the LORD will not lead me into temptation, but He will deliver me from evil, in Jesus' name.

2. Under the covering of the Superior Blood of Jesus the Christ, I pray that the LORD will strengthen my spirit being, and ignite the fire of the Holy Ghost in me.

3. Under the covering of the Superior Blood of Jesus the Christ, I pray that I will operate with divine wisdom and counsel before any act of faith, in Jesus' name.

4. Under the covering of the Superior Blood of Jesus the Christ, I pray for the spirit of discernment to understand the operations and wiles of the devil, in Jesus' name.

5. Under the covering of the Superior Blood of Jesus the Christ, I pray for a heart of service and faithfulness unto the LORD.

6. Under the covering of the Superior Blood of Jesus the Christ, I pray that the LORD will give me a desire and a love for His Word and Prayer.

7. Under the covering of the Superior Blood of Jesus the Christ, I pray for the Word of Knowledge and

the Word of Wisdom to know what is the acceptable will of the Father for me.

8. Under the covering of the Superior Blood of Jesus the Christ, I pray for the Gifts of the Holy Spirit so I can mature and grow in the wondrous grace of the Spirit.

9. Under the covering of the Superior Blood of Jesus the Christ, I pray for the Fruit of the Spirit to strengthen me spiritually and to be an asset to other believers.

10. Under the covering of the Superior Blood of Jesus the Christ, I commit my works to Him and my thoughts are established in Him.

11. Under the covering of the Superior Blood of Jesus the Christ, I boldly confess and declare, I do not take God for granted, for before I do anything or go anywhere, I acknowledge him so as to walk by divine direction.

12. Under the covering of the Superior Blood of Jesus the Christ, I boldly confess and declare, I am committed to an obedience lifestyle.

LOG-OFF: EVENING PRAYER

Enter and make these declarations over your life and church (pray each point at least 5 minutes; this is will give you a total of at least 60minutes in evening prayer).

1. Under the covering of the Superior Blood of Jesus the Christ, O LORD, I vow from today that I am not reserving any part of myself, my possessions, my energy and time from you because I am now aware of the plan that you have for me and I am willing to do what you expect of me.

2. Under the covering of the Superior Blood of Jesus the Christ, O LORD, I know that if I make less than 100-percent surrender to you, the devil will take advantage of any space I leave to make in road into that uncommitted area of my life.

3. Under the covering of the Superior Blood of Jesus the Christ, I am totally surrendered to the Father of spirits. He is my all in all, in Jesus' name.

4. Under the covering of the Superior Blood of Jesus the Christ, I am willing to place my trust in the wisdom and the will of God.

5. Under the covering of the Superior Blood of Jesus the Christ, LORD, I thank you for the commitment I have to help members of my physical and spiritual families.

6. Under the covering of the Superior Blood of Jesus the Christ, I declare with the help of God, I will be committed to my pastor and church, especially his welfare and the progress of the ministry.

7. Under the covering of the Superior Blood of Jesus the Christ, I vow and declare to be committed to the fellowship of the church in Jesus' name.

8. Under the covering of the Superior Blood of Jesus the Christ, I destroy the forces responsible for every lack of commitment in my life up until now. Henceforth, anything I start, I am committed to finish it, in Jesus' name.

9. Under the covering of the Superior Blood of Jesus the Christ, Anything I say, I am committed to doing it, in Jesus' name.

10. Under the covering of the Superior Blood of Jesus the Christ, Anything I do I am committed to being my best. I receive fresh grace for commitment, in Jesus' name.

11. Under the covering of the Superior Blood of Jesus the Christ, I pray that our church workers receive divine strength to be committed to their duties in Jesus' name.

12. Under the covering of the Superior Blood of Jesus the Christ, I will not abandon the duties committed into my hands by God and for my oversight.

DAY 29

The Response To The Temptations [Luke 4: 4,8,12,13]

How do we win the battle for our destiny? We must understand what Jesus did, and we must do the same.

Take Note:

1. Jesus rebuked satan. [v.v.4,8,12].

> ➤ Don't sit in your temptation with the concept that it is the LORD who wants you to be tempted.

> ➤ Jesus fasted during His temptation to hasten His breakthrough. You can do likewise.

> ➤ Jesus rebuked the devil, fought back and won the victory. You must always pray and declare and decree to the devil that God has granted you the victory and you shall not forfeit it.

➤ Jesus proved His knowledge of Scriptures by decoding every lie of satan with a proven scripture. The best prayer is already recorded in the Bible. Read and pray.

2. Satan relinquishes for a season [Luke 4:13]

➤ Rebuke the devil and he shall flee from you. Open your mouth whenever you are trialed and tempted by the devil and he will surely recoil into his shell. Resist him with all vigor and force, and silence every word of negativity you hear in your mind and spirit.

➤ The same Jesus who won the battle in the wilderness against satan, said unto us His church, that He has given all power unto us. May we also overpower the enemy as our LORD did.

➤ Come boldly to the throne; and take your rightful place of authority as an overcomer.

➤ Satan will prey upon your ignorance but never on your divine insurance.

LOG-ON: MORNING PRAYER

Enter and make these declarations over your life and church (pray each point at least 5 minutes; this is will give you a total of at least 60 minutes in morning prayer).

1. Under the covering of the Superior Blood of Jesus the Christ, Pray against every voice of iniquity in Jesus' name.

2. Under the covering of the Superior Blood of Jesus the Christ, Pray and begin to rebuke the voice of accusation against your life, in Jesus' name.

3. Under the covering of the Superior Blood of Jesus the Christ, Pray and silence any voice of the tormentor, in Jesus' name.

4. Under the covering of the Superior Blood of Jesus the Christ, Pray and break every spirit of the pursuer against your life, in Jesus' name.

5. Under the covering of the Superior Blood of Jesus the Christ, Pray for divine rest and settlement, in Jesus' name.

6. Under the covering of the Superior Blood of Jesus the Christ, Pray to resist any diabolical attempt to use Scriptures to ensnare your destiny, in Jesus' name.

7. Under the covering of the Superior Blood of Jesus the Christ, Pray and release angels to chase out satan and his cohorts out of your life and family, in Jesus' name.

8. Under the covering of the Superior Blood of Jesus the Christ, I am committed to ensure that the vision of the local assembly is achieved at all costs.

9. Under the covering of the Superior Blood of Jesus the Christ, I believe and confess that the grace of God is sufficient for me.

10. Under the covering of the Superior Blood of Jesus the Christ, I boldly declare that everything I am and have is for the kingdom of God.

11. Under the covering of the Superior Blood of Jesus the Christ, My heart is yielded to do the will of God. His love fills my heart.

12. Under the covering of the Superior Blood of Jesus the Christ, I am anointed to operate in holy zeal.

LOG-OFF: EVENING PRAYER

Enter and make these declarations over your life and church (pray each point at least 5 minutes; this is will give you a total of at least 60 minutes in evening prayer).

1. Under the covering of the Superior Blood of Jesus the Christ, Beginning from this day, I employ the services of the angels of God to open unto me, my family, my church and pastors, every door of opportunity and breakthroughs, in the name of Jesus.

2. Under the covering of the Superior Blood of Jesus the Christ, I will not go around in circles again, our church families will make progress, in the name of Jesus.

3. Under the covering of the Superior Blood of Jesus the Christ, We shall not build for another to inhabit and We shall not plant for another to eat, in the name of Jesus.

4. Under the covering of the Superior Blood of Jesus the Christ, I paralyze the powers working against my fruitfulness, and the devourer of families in my local church, in the name of Jesus.

5. Under the covering of the Superior Blood of Jesus the Christ, Oh Lord, let every locust, caterpillar and palmer-worm assigned to eat the fruit of my labor and that of families in my local church be roasted by the fire of God.

6. Under the covering of the Superior Blood of Jesus the Christ, The enemy shall not spoil my testimony in this fasting season, in the name of Jesus.

7. Under the covering of the Superior Blood of Jesus the Christ, I reject every backward journey for myself and every member of my local church, in the name of Jesus.

8. Under the covering of the Superior Blood of Jesus the Christ, I paralyze every strongman (spirit of the oppressor) attached to any area of my life and anchored to any member of my local church, in the name of Jesus.

9. Under the covering of the Superior Blood of Jesus the Christ, Let every agent of shame fashioned to work against my life, my family and my local church be paralyzed, in the name of Jesus.

10. Under the covering of the Superior Blood of Jesus the Christ, I paralyze the activities of household wickedness (familiar spirits) over my life, in the name of Jesus.
11. Under the covering of the Superior Blood of Jesus the Christ, We quench every strange fire emanating from evil tongues against my life and my local church, in the name of Jesus.
12. Under the covering of the Superior Blood of Jesus the Christ, Lord, give us power in my local church for maximum achievement.

DAY 30

Power And Influence After Fasting [Luke 4:14,15,23]

What happened in the life of Jesus after His 40-day fast is a direct testament of what will happen to any believer who fasts. Fasting brings the powerful influence of the Holy Spirit upon your life. It will impart the awesome presence of God upon your life. You'll operate in the Giftings of the Holy Spirit, and your influence will increase due to the activity of God's power in your life. People will be attracted to the glory on you, and lives will be transformed.

Take Note:

1. Powerful. [Luke 4:14,23].

> ➤ This season of fasting will release power into your life.

> ➤ After every fast, power is made available in matchless grace.

> ➤ The most important and yet priceless commodity on earth is power. It is said that, "if you hear that someone's is selling Power, sell your mother and buy it. After you gain the Power, use it to release your mother."

> ➤ Dr. Luke, informed us that Jesus went into the fast, filled with and led by the Spirit (Luke 4:1), but returned from the fast under the power of the Spirit. (Luke 4:14).

> ➤ You went into this fast hopeless, but you shall return from it hopeful.

> ➤ You went into this fast discouraged, but you shall return with courage.

> ➤ You went into this fast powerless, but you shall return with power.

> ➤ You went into this fast sick, but you shall return healed.

> You went into this fast depressed, but you shall return pressing forward.

2. Popular [Luke 4:14,15]

> He went into the wilderness (into isolation, incubation, and out of sight), yet He returned into fame, and popularity. Dr. Luke said, "...and there went out a fame of Him through all the region round about." May this be your portion in Jesus' name.

> The wilderness is a place of unfruitfulness, but He returned into the land of fruitfulness. May this fast end with you in a place of elevation and fruitfulness.

> As the fame of Jesus went abroad at the end of His fast, so may the Holy Spirit grant you favor and influence at every point of vantage, in Jesus' name.

> May God Almighty create room for your promotion at the end of this fast, even as He did for Jesus.

LOG-ON: MORNING PRAYER

Enter and make these declarations over your life and church (pray each point at least 5 minutes; this is will give you a total of at least 60 minutes in morning prayer).

1. Under the covering of the Superior Blood of Jesus the Christ, I pray for the power of the Holy Spirit to arrest and infect my lifestyle, in Jesus' name.

2. Under the covering of the Superior Blood of Jesus the Christ, I pray for the power Gifts of the Holy Spirit to be manifested in my life, in Jesus' name.

3. Under the covering of the Superior Blood of Jesus the Christ, I pray that I will exercise power over demonic entities and associates of darkness, in Jesus' name.

4. Under the covering of the Superior Blood of Jesus the Christ, I pray that my tongue shall be like fire, that whatever I speak shall carry the full force of the Holy Ghost fire, in Jesus' name.

5. Under the covering of the Superior Blood of Jesus the Christ, I pray that none of my words will fall to the ground, but I shall decree a thing and it shall be performed, in Jesus' name.

6. Under the covering of the Superior Blood of Jesus the Christ, I pray that the gates of hades shall hear and obey my voice, in Jesus' name.

7. Under the covering of the Superior Blood of Jesus the Christ, I pray that the Holy Ghost will enhance

my voice to carry authority and potency over devils, in Jesus' name.

8. Under the covering of the Superior Blood of Jesus the Christ, I pray that like Jabez and Jesus, God's fame will work through me to reach the outmost parts of the world, in Jesus' name.

9. Under the covering of the Superior Blood of Jesus the Christ, I pray that God will use me to affect someone this year in Jesus' name.

10. Under the covering of the Superior Blood of Jesus the Christ, I pray that my purpose shall manifest and it will be fulfilled, in Jesus' name.

11. Under the covering of the Superior Blood of Jesus the Christ, I pray that I shall not die but I will leave to declare the Word of God concerning my life, in Jesus' name.

12. Under the covering of the Superior Blood of Jesus the Christ, I pray that I will be an asset and a positive addition to my church this year, in Jesus' name.

LOG-OFF: EVENING PRAYER

Enter and make these declarations over your life and church (pray each point at least 5 minutes; this is will give you a total of at least 60 minutes in evening prayer).

1. Under the covering of the Superior Blood of Jesus the Christ, O Lord! I lift up my eyes to your Holy Hills, where my help comes from; And I declare today, incline your ear unto me, and hasten your help toward me in this my trouble, in Jesus' name – PRAY...

2. Under the covering of the Superior Blood of Jesus the Christ, O Lord, I confess and believe that you are the creator of the Heavens and the Earth, you control the affairs of men and the universe, I now submit myself for Divine control and supervision. Pilot my life O Lord, and lead me to the still waters in, Jesus' name – PRAY...

3. Under the covering of the Superior Blood of Jesus the Christ, You kept Israel, and did not slumber nor sleep, order my feet not to be moved in this my distress; strengthen me, uphold me, and cause any demonic satellite devices watching over my life to catch afire now, in Jesus' name – PRAY ...

4. Under the covering of the Superior Blood of Jesus the Christ, O Lord, I submit that you're the keeper of my life, now cause any networks of demonic eyes, crystal balls, magic mirrors, and sorcery monitoring my life to be destroyed by Your consuming fire now, in Jesus' name – PRAY...

5. Under the covering of the Superior Blood of Jesus the Christ, Any demonic influence that works with the energy of the sun to destroy my life and to smite me by day; obey the Word of the Lord, and terminate now, in Jesus' name. PRAY...

6. Under the covering of the Superior Blood of Jesus the Christ, Any occult mysticism that employs the power of the moon to interrupt my destiny, receive fire now and face utter destruction, in Jesus' name. PRAY...

7. Under the covering of the Superior Blood of Jesus the Christ, I Command the sun and the moon to favor my cause, and work in my favor, in Jesus' name. (Isaiah 45:11)...PRAY

8. Under the covering of the Superior Blood of the Living Christ, I confess and believe that I am shielded, protected, and defended against any demonic assaults, counterattacks, charms, curses and divinations and enchantments, in Jesus' name. (3x)....PRAY

9. Under the covering of the Superior Blood of Jesus the Christ, O Lord, preserve my soul from soul-robbers and demonic soul-ties. I lock myself under thy control, steer my going in and my coming out from this time forth and forever more, in Jesus' name. PRAY...

10. Under the covering of the Superior Blood of Jesus the Christ, O Lord, I boldly confess and believe that You are my hiding place; you will protect me from trouble and surround me with songs of deliverance, in Jesus' name. PRAY...

11. Under the covering of the Superior Blood of Jesus the Christ, My LORD, protect me and preserve my life; Bless me in this land and do not surrender me to the desire of my foes, in Jesus' name. PRAY...

12. Under the covering of the Superior Blood of the Living Christ, I acknowledge that this year no harm will befall me, no disaster will come near my tent, in Jesus' name. PRAY...

DAY 31

Purposeful [Luke 4:15 ...taught...]

The destiny of Jesus was ignited by fasting and prayer. He began His ministry with fasting, signifying to the believer that regarding anything God has commissioned us to do here on earth, we can only be successful by starting with fasting. The disciples (later known as the apostles) took this lesson from Jesus, and commenced their ministry by spending ten days, fasting and praying in the Upper room. Paul upon his calling and experience on the road to Damascus mentions that he spent three years in a secluded place seeking the face of God in fasting and prayer. Later, he will declare that he is "fasting often." He had greater results because he made fasting a lifestyle. Looking through the scriptures, from Genesis to Revelation, anyone who God commissioned, began their journey with fasting. Fasting reveals and initiates divine purpose.

Take Note:

> ➤ Jesus returned in wisdom and with influence. The people were astonished by His exposition into the Divine Word. May you increase in wisdom and influence as this fast draws to a close.

> ➤ He went into the fast without purpose, but in those days, He fasted and did not return until purpose was materialized. If you are confused, depressed, and stagnant in your life, may this fast hasten your breakthrough and release your purpose, in Jesus' name.

> ➤ He taught with authority such as the people had never seen before. I pray that this fast may elevate you in the things of God. May your authority be unchallenged at the gates; and may you be the mouthpiece of God this year. May springs of water flow through you by the doings of the Holy Spirit.

> ➤ Let this fasting create in you the spirit of a soul winner and a kingdom propagator.

> ➤ If you have lost purpose and vision, may this fasting season release your inner sight, unstop your earring, and open your sensitivity to recognize and fulfill purpose.

> ➤ Fasting brings divine directions and divine enforcement of God's purpose.

LOG-ON: MORNING PRAYER

Enter and make these declarations over your life and church (pray each point at least 5 minutes; this is will give you a total of at least 60 minutes in morning prayer).

1. Under the covering of the Superior Blood of Jesus the Christ, I shall not die unfulfilled, in Jesus' name.
2. Under the covering of the Superior Blood of Jesus the Christ, My father and my God, bring all my prayers to pass at the right time, in Jesus' name.
3. Under the covering of the Superior Blood of Jesus the Christ, O Lord arise, in Jesus' name and answer all my prayers.
4. Under the covering of the Superior Blood of Jesus the Christ, O God instruct me on what to do with my........in Jesus name. **Pick from the list**: Business, Marriage, Finances, Health, and Destiny etc.
5. Under the covering of the Superior Blood of Jesus the Christ, O God reveal to me on what to do with my............in Jesus' name. **Pick from the list**: Business, Marriage, Finances, Health, and Destiny, etc.
6. Under the covering of the Superior Blood of Jesus the Christ, I will walk in the path of God, in Jesus' name.
7. Under the covering of the Superior Blood of Jesus the Christ, My Father and my God, bring all my prayers to pass at the right time, in Jesus' name.
8. Under the covering of the Superior Blood of Jesus the Christ, O Lord arise, in Jesus' name and answer all my prayers.

9. Under the covering of the Superior Blood of Jesus the Christ, O LORD arise and lift up my head, in Jesus' name.

10. Under the covering of the Superior Blood of Jesus the Christ, My Father and my God, bring all my prayers to pass at the right time in Jesus name.

11. Under the covering of the Superior Blood of Jesus the Christ, My LORD, be with me and watch over me wherever I go, and bring me back to the place of my habitation. Do not leave me and do what You have promised me, in Jesus' name.

12. Under the covering of the Superior Blood of Jesus the Christ, I speak to my soul, why are you distressed? Awake; why are you afraid? Gather up your strength; why fear their threats and conspiracies? I have set the LORD always before me. Because He is at my right hand, I will not be shaken, in Jesus' name.

LOG-OFF: EVENING PRAYER

Enter and make these declarations over your life and church (pray each point at least 5 minutes; this is will give you a total of at least 60 minutes in evening prayer).

1. Under the covering of the Superior Blood of Jesus the Christ, O Lord, send forth labourers into Your vineyard, to reach the unreached in this country.

2. Under the covering of the Superior Blood of Jesus the Christ, I command the consuming fire of God, on all idols, sacrifices, rituals, shrines and local satanic thrones in this country, in Jesus' name.

3. Under the covering of the Superior Blood of Jesus the Christ, I break, any conscious and unconscious agreement made between the people of this country and satan, in Jesus' name.

4. Under the covering of the Superior Blood of Jesus the Christ, I break any covenant between any satanic external influence and our leaders, in the name of Jesus.

5. Under the covering of the Superior Blood of Jesus the Christ, I paralyze every spirit of wastage of economic resources in this country, in the name of Jesus.

6. Under the covering of the Superior Blood of Jesus the Christ, O Lord, show Yourself mighty, in the affairs of this nation.

7. Under the covering of the Superior Blood of Jesus the Christ, Let the kingdom of Christ come into this nation, in Jesus' name.

8. Under the covering of the Superior Blood of Jesus the Christ, O Lord, do new things in our country, to show Your power and greatness to the heathen.
9. Under the covering of the Superior Blood of Jesus the Christ, Let the kingdom of our Lord Jesus Christ come into the heart of every person in this country, in the name of Jesus.
10. Under the covering of the Superior Blood of Jesus the Christ, O Lord, have mercy upon this nation.
11. Under the covering of the Superior Blood of Jesus the Christ, Let all the glory of this nation, that has departed be restored, in the name of Jesus.
12. Under the covering of the Superior Blood of Jesus the Christ, Let all un-evangelized areas of this country be reached with the Gospel of our Lord Jesus Christ, in the name of Jesus.

DAY 32

Intercessory Prayer

You'll enlist with God on behalf of the Earth to be an intercessor for Church crisis. You'll devote this whole day praying for the topic indicated in the crisis. As you intercede on behalf humanity, may Heaven speedily answer your personal prayer request. May Almighty God do for you, even as you pray for others. As a point of contact, you may mention the names of people you know who specifically petition God for deliverance.

INTERCESSOR:

TIME:

Theme: The Mission Is Not Impossible

Scripture: "But Jesus beheld them, and said unto them, With men this is impossible; but with God all things are possible." – Mathew 19:26

"Verily, verily, I say unto you, He that believeth on me, the works that I do shall he do also; and greater works than these shall he do; because I go unto my Father." – John 14:12.

Problem: Fatherlessness, The Cancer Epidemic of Our Culture – I realize that "Epidemic" and the "C word" are strong, but they are not strong enough to depict what is going on in our nation and people are not speaking of it. It is politically incorrect to speak of the fatherless epidemic because it infers that a two-parent family is superior to a single parent family. However difficult it is to speak of, it must be addressed because every social problem in our culture, from poverty to crimes, such as school shootings have fatherlessness as a major contributing factor. Consider these statistics:

Children from fatherless homes are:

- 4.6 times more likely to commit suicide,
- 6.6 times more likely to become teenaged mothers (if they are girls, of course),
- 24.3 times more likely to run away,
- 15.3 times more likely to have behavioral disorders,
- 6.3 times more likely to be in a state-operated institution,
- 10.8 times more likely to commit rape,
- 6.6 times more likely to drop out of school,
- 15.3 times more likely to end up in prison while a teenager. [*Source: Current Populations Reports, US Bureau of the Census, Series P-20, No. 458, 1991].*

- 26 out of 27 deadliest mass shooters in the United States, came from broken families with no biological dad, an absent father, an abusive father or a divorced parent at home. Statistics show that the common denominator for the majority of these mass shooters is the absence of a father.
- 15.3 times more likely to end up in prison while a teenager.
- The relationship between family structure and crime is so strong that controlling for family configuration erases the relationship between race and crime and between low income and crime. This conclusion shows up time and again in literature. [*Source: E. Kamarck, William Galston, Putting Children First, Progressive Policy Inst. 1990*].

Assignment: Fatherlessness is growing out of control and it is destroying the nurturing building block of our society; the family. The results are increased crime, poverty and very unhappy, floundering children. There's a curse in a home without a father, and a fatherless nation is under a curse. Prophet Malachi record that in order for there to be a revival, God must restore the role of fathers:

> "*And he shall turn the heart of the fathers to the children, and the heart of the children to their fathers, lest I come*

and smite the earth with
a curse," Malachi 4:6.

Before this, Prophet Jeremiah had already recorded how Jerusalem was ruined and the lives of the young men were wasted because there were no fathers at the gates:

> *The elders have gone*
> *from the gate, the young*
> *men from their music.*
> *(Lamentation 5:14).*

Pray that God will fulfill the promise in Malachi 4:6, and restore the heart of the fathers to the children, and vice-versa. Pray that we'll see a revival of the restoration of our homes, in Jesus' name.

Duration:

CHAPTER 7
WEEK FIVE: I PRAYED

*And it came to pass, when I heard these words, that I …**prayed before***
***the God of heaven**.*
– Nehemiah 1:4

7

WEEK FIVE – I Prayed

These final 8 days complete our 40-day fasting period. I will like to sum up what the LORD has invited us to do this 40-day period. Let's go back to Nehemiah and recap the first and second chapter.

The end of chapter 1 records the horn of the dilemma. Nehemiah tells us he was cupbearer to the Persian emperor, Artaxerxes, the most powerful man in the world. Cupbearer was a very high station, an influential political position. Nehemiah had regular access to the king and would have been counted on to give advice. He surely had the status and wealth that went along with having such a position. His two identities pulled at him: brother to the exiles and cupbearer to the king.

Many of us are familiar with this tension. It may be that you're overcoming some pattern in your life that has ruined and hurt you, and this struggle is the pattern of stress you're called to live with. Or it may be that there is some other pressure upon you, a family crisis or medical emergency. Nehemiah's prayers and growing faith can be an encouragement in these circumstances as well. But those who have dual identities as Nehemiah did will find this chapter especially helpful.

We might note that others in the Bible faced the same problem Nehemiah did. Joseph had risen to the highest station of the land in Egypt, second only to Pharaoh, and he had to resolve the question of his identity as a Jew and his identity as an Egyptian. How would he serve God, having the place and opportunity that he did? David also had the same problem when he was running for his life from Saul. He lived for a time among the Philistines and was accorded a position of respect among them. Daniel who was Nebuchadnezzar's most important advisor, was also faced with the dichotomy. Likewise, Esther who served as queen in a Persian court. Her uncle Mordecai spoke to her at a crisis moment and said, "...Who knows but that you have come to royal position for such a time as this?" (Esther 4:14.) She was a Jewish believer, and she was queen in Persia. How would she resolve the dual responsibilities?

There are a couple of ways that most of us tend to react when we feel this sort of tension. Some of us, and I think this would have been Nehemiah's natural response, tend to fire off in all directions at once. If there are people suffering, somebody ought to do something about it. "I'm going to make some phone calls, issue a series of edicts, plan some strategies, and make something happen!" A lot of activity is generated, but nothing gets changed. The other natural inclination when we feel this vise of conflicting pressures, is to look at how hard it will be to do anything. It's such a long way from Susa to Jerusalem. The people have been there a long time, and they've got it tough, but what can be done? There's so much inertia to overcome, so many complexities and questions that need to be answered. So we decide somebody else ought to do it anyway. It's easy to be impressed with how difficult the problem is and just give up.

But Nehemiah didn't choose either of those natural options. What he did was enter into the presence of God in a profound way, and that's what we want to consider again as we end our 40 days of fasting.

Prayer Before The God of Heaven

*And it came to pass, when I heard these words, that I sat down and wept, and mourned certain days, and fasted, and **prayed before the God of heaven**. – Nehemiah 1:4*

The fifth thing mentioned in Nehemiah 1:4 is prayer before the God of heaven. That's a broad, inclusive term for communication with God. Knowing he had a problem, he spoke with and listened to the God of heaven, the Lord of all. His heart would not let him rest. He didn't know what to do, and so he spent these four months wrestling with God, calling on God, appealing, listening, returning, not settling for easy, obvious answers, but wanting to know what his Lord would do with his life, what his future should be.

Now we come to what I believe is a distillation of the prayer that occurred during the life of some of God's great servants. These individuals, as we'll observed through the final 8 days of the fast, changed their world.

Now we come to what I believe is a distillation of the prayer that occurred during those four months.

A prayer to the God who keeps his promises

Verses 5-11:

> *And said, I beseech you,*
> *O LORD God of*
> *heaven, the great and*
> *terrible God, that keeps*
> *covenant and mercy for*
> *them that love him and*
> *observe his*
> *commandments: Let*
> *your ear now be*
> *attentive, and your eyes*
> *open, that you may hear*

the prayer of your
servant, which I pray
before you now, day and
night, for the children of
Israel your servants, and
confess the sins of the
children of Israel, which
we have sinned against
you: both I and my
father's house have
sinned. We have dealt
very corruptly against
you, and have not kept
the commandments, nor
the statutes, nor the
judgments, which you
commanded your
servant Moses.
Remember, I beseech
you, the word that you
commanded your
servant Moses, saying, If
you transgress, I will
scatter you abroad
among the nations: But
if you turn to me, and
keep my
commandments, and do
them; though there were
of you cast out to the
uttermost part of the
heaven, yet will I gather
them from there, and

*will bring them to the
place that I have chosen
to set my name there.
Now these are your
servants and your
people, whom you have
redeemed by your great
power, and by your
strong hand. O LORD,
I beseech you, let now
your ear be attentive to
the prayer of your
servant, and to the
prayer of your servants,
who desire to fear your
name: and prosper, I
pray you, your servant
this day, and grant him
mercy in the sight of this
man. For I was the
king's cupbearer..*

I want to urge upon us that we can know what the LORD
wants from us. When things seem confusing, when
pressures pull us in more than one direction regarding
where we should be and who we should be and how we
should use our gifts and what ministry we should have and
how and when? The way to find our answers to these
questions is the pattern of Nehemiah: to spend this focused,
honest, lengthy, serious time with God.

His choice was to say, "Lord, direct me. Make of me what
you want. I'm willing to invest myself in pursuing you to

find out." If you're experiencing the same longing to know what God would make of your life, are you willing to do what Nehemiah did? Are you willing to spend this kind of time with God with this level of passion, this level of love and expectancy?

We learn a lot about Nehemiah by looking at the kind of prayer he prayed. When Nehemiah first heard about the ruin of Jerusalem, he prayed for four months. This isn't casual, off-hand prayer. This prayer gives us a pattern for successful praying. If you want to know how to pray, study the book of Nehemiah and particularly this prayer.

With that in mind, we'll finish our final eight days with:

The Four Elements of Prayer Taken From the Life of Nehemiah
1. Focus On What God Can; Not What You Can.
2. Confess Your Failure, to Confirm God's Authority.
3. Recall God's Faithfulness To Rely on God's Promises.
4. The Prayer of Specification Is A Quick Antidote to Delayed Situations.

The Four Important Specific Qualities to Nehemiah's Prayer
1. It's a Prayer of Adoration
2. It's a Prayer of Admission
3. It's a Prayer of Assurance
4. It's a Prayer of Action

May these last eight days be the greatest in your life so far, in Jesus' name.

DAY 33

Focus On What God Can; Not What You Can

The only limitation on prayer is what you say and what you see. God said to Abraham, "as far as your eyes can see" I give unto you. The limitation was not on God's part; God was willing to give as far as Abraham could see. This places the limit to what God can do, on what Abraham could see. If we focus on our capabilities, our strength, our finances, and our relationships, we'll not see far enough. We must focus on God's abilities, God's strength, His faithfulness, and His unlimited power. Paul said, "my God shall supply all your needs, according to His riches in heavenly places." How can "all" our needs be supplied? We must focus not on our bank account, but on the unlimited resources of God.

Moreover, we focus on God because of who God is. We focus on God because God is a faithful God, a great God, a loving God, a wonderful God. God can handle anything!

In verse 5, Nehemiah says, *"O LORD, God of heaven, the great and awesome God who keeps his covenant of unfailing love with those who love him and obey his commands."*

Nehemiah said a couple things about God right up front:
    a. You're great and awesome - that declares God's power.
    b. You keep your promises – that honors God's covenant and affirms God's faithfulness.

Nehemiah acknowledges who God is and how great and worthy God is. That's what praise is. Acknowledge who God is and His greatness. Nehemiah knows that the problems in Jerusalem are great but that God is greater. It's a big mess, but God is bigger than any mess. He has the right focus and perspective. It's based on God's character. As you go through this day, focus on what God can, and not on what you can.

LOG-ON: MORNING PRAYER

Enter and make these declarations over your life and church (pray each point at least 5 minutes; this is will give you a total of at least 60 minutes in morning prayer).

1. Under the covering of the Superior Blood of Jesus the Christ, That which is bigger than what money and my family can buy – release it for me oh LORD!

2. Under the covering of the Superior Blood of Jesus the Christ, God, all that I have, my money, my brains, my strength, etc. – use it for Your Glory oh LORD!

3. Under the covering of the Superior Blood of Jesus the Christ, Where no one has ever been to, what no one has ever touched in my lineage, let divine arrangement take me there.

4. Under the covering of the Superior Blood of Jesus the Christ, Father, in every area of my life, make me exceptional!

5. Under the covering of the Superior Blood of Jesus the Christ, Lord, I do not want to be physically taller, arrange an uncommon spiritual height for me! Let me grow in the spirit.

6. Under the covering of the Superior Blood of Jesus the Christ, on the day that promotion is arranged, let me be selected for the position.

7. Under the covering of the Superior Blood of Jesus the Christ, Lord, let today be my day of visitation, in Jesus' name.

8. Under the covering of the Superior Blood of Jesus the Christ, as I step out of this prayer session, I receive a divine exposure to greatness!
9. Under the covering of the Superior Blood of Jesus the Christ, let my legs walk me into a divine encounter this week.
10. Under the covering of the Superior Blood of Jesus the Christ, I decree concerning my life, all my setbacks will be arranged to favor me!
11. Under the covering of the Superior Blood of Jesus the Christ, let every setback in my life be utilized by God for my divine coronation into greatness.
12. Under the covering of the Superior Blood of Jesus the Christ, Lord, while the power of divine arrangement is working behind the scene, let me not be broken-down in Jesus' name!

LOG-OFF: EVENING PRAYER

Enter and make these declarations over your life and church (pray each point at least 5 minutes; this is will give you a total of at least 60 minutes in evening prayer).

1. Under the covering of the Superior Blood of Jesus the Christ, Oh God, release a helper into my life who will support my walk into divine purpose!
2. Under the covering of the Superior Blood of Jesus the Christ, Oh God, let my pains push me to you! Let my cries be heard in Heaven!
3. Under the covering of the Superior Blood of Jesus the Christ, Oh God, make me a source of help to people who need divine connections.
4. Under the covering of the Superior Blood of Jesus the Christ, every demonic and evil plan intended to derail me, STOP, in Jesus' name.
5. Under the covering of the Superior Blood of Jesus the Christ, I decree that I will not take that step that will make me miss or walk away from divine purpose.
6. Under the covering of the Superior Blood of Jesus the Christ, Oh God, every plan that you have been working for me, FAST TRACK it – let it manifest today!
7. Under the covering of the Superior Blood of Jesus the Christ, Oh God, the one whom you have planned to help me – talk to him or her today.

8. Under the covering of the Superior Blood of Jesus the Christ, Oh God, no matter how far away they are, the one you have ordained to pull me up – speak to him or loud and clear today!
9. Under the covering of the Superior Blood of Jesus the Christ, every helper who is in the divine plan for my future – manifest!
10. Under the covering of the Superior Blood of Jesus the Christ, every power blocking the plans Heaven has made for me – be destroyed today permanently in Jesus name!
11. Under the covering of the Superior Blood of Jesus the Christ, Lord! Oh God, speak now that my tomorrow will be brighter and alright!
12. Under the covering of the Superior Blood of Jesus the Christ, send me Lord to where the arrangement that will give me rest has been made, in the name of Jesus!

DAY 34

Confess Your Failure, To Confirm God's Authority

The people had disobeyed God. As a result, God had said, "If you don't obey me you're going to lose the land I gave you." And they did lose it and were taken into foreign captivity all because they had disobeyed God.

In verses 6 and 7 Nehemiah prays:

> "...I confess that we
> have sinned against you.
> Yes, even my own family
> and I have sinned! We
> have sinned terribly by
> not obeying the
> commands, decrees, and
> regulations that you
> gave us through your
> servant Moses."

So he based his request on who God is and that God is worthy; but he also had to admit things about who he was and that he was unworthy; that he was part of the problem. He doesn't talk about others being bad he talks about himself and his family. Even when he talks about the people, he includes himself by saying "we." He says things like, "I confess... *we have sinned... my own family and I... We have sinned terribly... not obeying the commands... you gave us.*" It wasn't Nehemiah's fault they had been taken into captivity. He hadn't even been born when it happened. Yet, he includes himself. He says "I'm part of the problem".

There's personal confession, group confession, community confession and there's national confession. In America we're individualistic in how we look at things. We act like if I didn't actually do the specific thing that started something, then I have no responsibility. That's not Biblical. In our culture I'm taught to confess my sins. When was the last time you confessed the sins of the nation... or the sins of your family... or your church... or your group of friends... or of your cultural or social group? We don't think that way. Our society has taught us that you are only responsible for you. And that's just not true! You are your brother's keeper. We are all in this together.

One phrase I hate hearing is "I've got to do what's best for me!" All kinds of things get justified with that phrase. Nehemiah shows in his prayer that not only do we have personal sin to confess but we have corporate sin. We are part of any sin of our culture; we are part of any sin that is part of our heritage; we are part of any sin where we benefit from the results of someone else's loss, even if we weren't one of those who caused us to have that benefit. Authentic believers accept the blame.

Our prayer today should be, *"We have sinned against you."*

We confess that we are part of the problem, and that God has the right and authority to hold us accountable. The point is that all sin is ultimately against God. David said, *"Against you, and you alone, have I sinned; I have done what is evil in your sight. You will be proved right in what you say, and your judgment against me is just."* He knew and acknowledged that sin is against God and that God has the authority to hold us responsible for it.

LOG-ON: MORNING PRAYER

Enter and make these declarations over your life and church (pray each point at least 5 minutes; this is will give you a total of at least 60 minutes in morning prayer).

1. Under the covering of the Superior Blood of Jesus the Christ, I repent for the church of Christ for bearing the vessel of the Lord with unclean hands. Father, forgive us.
2. Under the covering of the Superior Blood of Jesus the Christ, I repent for the church of Christ for

kindling strange fires before the Lord. Father, forgive us.

3. Under the covering of the Superior Blood of Jesus the Christ, I repent for the church of Christ for turning the house of the Lord into the den of thieves. Father, forgive us in the name of Jesus Christ.

4. Under the covering of the Superior Blood of Jesus the Christ, I repent for the church of Christ for soiling the name of the Lord. Father, forgive us.

5. Under the covering of the Superior Blood of Jesus the Christ, I repent for the church of Christ for preaching another gospel. Father, forgive us in Jesus' name.

6. Under the covering of the Superior Blood of Jesus the Christ, I repent for the church of Christ for bringing worldliness into the church. Father, forgive us in Jesus' name.

7. Under the covering of the Superior Blood of Jesus the Christ, I repent for the church of Christ for not evangelizing. Father, forgive us in Jesus' name.

8. Under the covering of the Superior Blood of Jesus the Christ, I repent for the church of Christ for not preparing the people of Christ for rapture. Father, forgive us in Jesus' name.

9. Under the covering of the Superior Blood of Jesus the Christ, I repent for the church of Christ for following after other gods. Father, forgive us in Jesus' name.

10. Under the covering of the Superior Blood of Jesus the Christ, I repent for the church of Christ for quenching the fire of Holy Ghost. Father, forgive us in Jesus' name.

11. Under the covering of the Superior Blood of Jesus the Christ, I repent for the church of Christ for quenching the fires of God's altar. Father, forgive us in Jesus name.

12. Under the covering of the Superior Blood of Jesus the Christ, I repent for the church of Christ for turning the altars of God into ruins. Father, forgive us in Jesus' name.

LOG-OFF: EVENING PRAYER

Enter and make these declarations over your life and church (pray each point at least 5 minutes; this is will give you a total of at least 60 minutes in evening prayer).

1. Under the covering of the Superior Blood of Jesus the Christ, I repent for the church of Christ for turning the altars of God into ruins. Father, forgive us in Jesus' name.

2. Under the covering of the Superior Blood of Jesus the Christ, I repent for the church of Christ for false prophecies. Father, forgive us in Jesus' name.

3. Under the covering of the Superior Blood of Jesus the Christ, I repent for the church of Christ for preaching half truth. Father, forgive us in Jesus' name.

4. Under the covering of the Superior Blood of Jesus the Christ, I repent for the church of Christ for condoning sins. Father, forgive us in Jesus' name.

5. Under the covering of the Superior Blood of Jesus the Christ, I repent for the church of Christ for denominationalism. Father, forgive us in Jesus' name.

6. Under the covering of the Superior Blood of Jesus the Christ, I repent for the church of Christ for merchandising the gospel. Father, forgive us in Jesus' name.

7. Under the covering of the Superior Blood of Jesus the Christ, I repent for the church of Christ for introducing partisan politics into the church. Father, forgive us in Jesus' name.

8. Under the covering of the Superior Blood of Jesus the Christ, I repent for the church of Christ for not helping the poor, widows and orphans in the church.

9. Under the covering of the Superior Blood of Jesus the Christ, I repent for the church of Christ for using manipulations, necromancy, enchantments and divinations.

10. Under the covering of the Superior Blood of Jesus the Christ, I repent for the church of Christ for practicing witchcraft in the church. Father, forgive us in the name of Jesus Christ.

11. Under the covering of the Superior Blood of Jesus the Christ, I repent for the church of Christ for the hatred, envy and competition among ministers. Father, forgive us in Jesus' name.

12. Under the covering of the Superior Blood of Jesus the Christ, I repent for the church of Christ for adultery by and among ministers. Father, forgive us in Jesus' name.

DAY 35

Recall God's Faithfulness To Rely On God's Promises.

In verses 8-9, Nehemiah prayed, *"Please remember what you told your servant Moses: 'If you are unfaithful to me, I will scatter you among the nations. But if you return to me and obey my commands and live by them, then even if you are exiled to the ends of the earth, I will bring you back to the place I have chosen for my name to be honored."*

Notice He says "if ... I will" It's a warning and a promise.

Nehemiah prays to God and says, "I want you to remember what you told Moses." God warned us through Moses that if we were unfaithful, we would lose the land. But God also promised that if we repent He'd give it back to us. In the Bible you often find God's people reminding God about what He said He wants to do. David did it. Abraham, Moses and the prophets did it.

So does God need to be reminded? No of course not. Does God forget what he's promised? No. Then why do this? Because recounting it helps us remember and acknowledge what God has done and what God has promised. It pleases God when you remind God of one of His promises because that demonstrates that you're paying attention.

Part of prayer is taking God by using God's word. It's asking God to do what God's already promised and wants to do. God wants to bless you even more than you want to be blessed. But God sets things up so that you have to be part of it. You need to pray to experience the promises of God.

Nehemiah could go to God about these promises because he knew them. Parts of the promises he mentions in these verses come from several prophesies, including the prophesies of Jeremiah, some of them come from Leviticus 26:27-33 and Deuteronomy 30:4 - *"Even though you are banished to the ends of the earth, the Lord your God will gather you from there and bring you back again."* Nehemiah knew all of this, so he could pray as God intends for us to pray. The strength of my prayer life is measured by how well I know the promises and purposes of God. For that, we need to know the promises of God.

LOG-ON: MORNING PRAYER

Enter and make these declarations over your life and church (pray each point at least 5 minutes; this is will give you a total of at least 60 minutes in morning prayer).

1. Under the covering of the Superior Blood of Jesus the Christ, Thank You Father for Your faithfulness, because Your word says "faithful is He, that has promised". (Hebrews 10:23).

2. Under the covering of the Superior Blood of Jesus the Christ, Thank You Father for all Your unfailing promises over my life.

3. Under the covering of the Superior Blood of Jesus the Christ, Father, in any way that I have fallen short of Your glory, have mercy and forgive me.

4. Under the covering of the Superior Blood of Jesus the Christ, Father, let Your fire consume whatever is responsible for the delay in the manifestation of Your promises in my life.

5. Under the covering of the Superior Blood of Jesus the Christ, Father, let every Prince of Persia, preventing answers to my prayers from reaching me, be paralyzed, in Jesus' name.

6. Under the covering of the Superior Blood of Jesus the Christ, Father, let every "hard rock" of the enemies, at the bottom of the well of my breakthrough, be blasted to pieces, by Your thunder, in Jesus' name.

7. Under the covering of the Superior Blood of Jesus the Christ, Father let the anointing for greater works, which You have promised me, fall upon me and begin to manifest in my life and ministry.

8. Under the covering of the Superior Blood of Jesus the Christ, Father, let every anti – breakthrough decrees and curses, in operation in my life, be broken and destroyed, today, by the blood of Jesus.

9. Under the covering of the Superior Blood of Jesus the Christ, Father, let every weapon fashioned against my financial, material, academic, ministerial and marital breakthroughs, be rendered obsolete and of no consequence, in Jesus' name.

10. Under the covering of the Superior Blood of Jesus the Christ, Father, You are the One who opens a door that no man can shut, please, open unto me, perpetually, this day, the doors of Your prosperity and financial breakthrough, in Jesus' name.

11. Under the covering of the Superior Blood of Jesus the Christ, Father, please, my eyes are on You, fulfill all Your promises in my life, in Jesus' name.

12. Under the covering of the Superior Blood of Jesus the Christ, Covenant Keeping God, forgive me for anything I have done to delay my destiny and Your Word for my life. Fulfill Your Word in my life this year in Jesus' name. I declare, I shall not die, but I will live to fulfill Your Word, in Jesus' name.

LOG-OFF: EVENING PRAYER

Enter and make these declarations over your life and church (pray each point at least 5 minutes; this is will give you a total of at least 60 minutes in evening prayer).

1.   Under the covering of the Superior Blood of Jesus the Christ, My Father, I humbly plead for Your undeserved mercy upon my life, my church, my nation and world. Lord, help us to come before You with deep awareness that we deserve Your judgment far more than Your blessing. By Jesus' blood alone, we plead for Your merciful grace to revive and bless us once again.

2.   Under the covering of the Superior Blood of Jesus the Christ, My Father, please send overwhelming conviction of sin, deep brokenness and genuine repentance among Your people. Grant to us the true Godly sorrow that leads to repentance. Fill us with holy fear and reverence for Your name. Purify the Church for the Glorious Second Coming of Jesus Christ. Please prepare and cleanse us for a deeper intimate relationship with you and for a lifestyle of eternity with you.

3.   Under the covering of the Superior Blood of Jesus the Christ, Mighty God, please come upon our pastors and endow them with a burning desire for deep repentance. Fill them with dynamic power and renewed passion for You. Grant to them a mighty wall of protection from the world, the flesh and the devil.

4.   Under the covering of the Superior Blood of Jesus the Christ, Mighty God, grant to us a burning

hunger for You and a passion for fervent prayer. Help us draw near to You and seek You with all our hearts. Lord, cause us to hunger and thirst for You above all else. Help us lead our churches to become houses of prayer for all nations.

5. Under the covering of the Superior Blood of Jesus the Christ, Holy Father, please bring us to loving unity in our churches and a deep harmony between our churches. Help us tear down the strongholds of bickering and disunity that so ravage Your Church.

6. Under the covering of the Superior Blood of Jesus the Christ, Everlasting LORD, please fill us with a burning passion to pray for and witness to the lost. Cause our eyes to weep for souls that we may reap in joy.

7. Under the covering of the Superior Blood of Jesus the Christ, Faithful God, empower Your people with a burning passion for local and global missions. Grant to us a fiery zeal for planting new churches and witnessing the Good News. Please forgive us for our frequent lack of concern beyond "me and mine."

8. Under the covering of the Superior Blood of Jesus the Christ, LORD of the harvest, please call thousands into ministry, missions and Christian witness. Send forth a mighty flood of laborers into the harvest. If there's no one to send, then use me LORD.

9. Under the covering of the Superior Blood of Jesus the Christ, Covenant Keeping God, we ask You to deepen and purify our very motives in praying for revival and blessing. Lord, teach us to seek Your face and not just Your hand. Cause us to seek You

and not just Your comfort or blessing. Dear God, teach us to pray for Your glory and pleasure, not our own.

10. Under the covering of the Superior Blood of Jesus the Christ, Holy Father, we humbly ask for a mighty move of conviction and salvation in government leaders and others who influence culture. We ask You to pour out convicting, saving power upon our nation, city, colleges, universities, media networks and the Hollywood movie industry. We ask that you so move that millions will be converted to Christ in these strategic communities of cultural influence. If you can use anything LORD, use me.

11. Under the covering of the Superior Blood of Jesus the Christ, Righteous Lord, we ask You to send sweeping revival even if it takes hard times and great trials to prepare the soil of our hearts. Father, we pray not for shallow selfish ends, but for Your great glory and kingdom. Cause us to come to You in true humility, brokenness and contriteness of heart.

12. Under the covering of the Superior Blood of Jesus the Christ, Sovereign God, we ask You to rend the heavens and send forth Your awesome "manifest presence." We ask You to so move that over 1 billion souls worldwide will be saved in a single year. Cause Your glory to sweep the whole earth bringing unprecedented millions to Christ. We humbly ask You to move even greater than You did in any previous awakening. Blessed God, we pray for one last great harvest before the glorious return of Your Son. Purify Your Church, and then come Lord Jesus, come quickly!

DAY 36

The Prayer of Specification Is A Quick Antidote to Delayed Situations

Make specific requests. For one thing, if you make general prayers, how will you know if they are answered? For another, God already knows what's needed and knows what you want. Prayer isn't about informing God, it's about you being a part of what God is doing in your life and in the world around you. Specific prayers are prayers that you are involved in. General prayers are lazy - you're not bothering to think them through or get all that involved.

In verses 10-11 Nehemiah includes the who, what, and when. He says, *"The people you rescued by your great power and strong hand are your servants. O Lord, please hear my prayer! Listen to the prayers of those of us who delight in honoring you. Please grant me success today by making the king favorable to me. Put it into his heart to be kind to me."*

Nehemiah has the whole prayer just to have that one little request at the end: *"Please grant me success today by making the king favorable to me."*

Nehemiah was willing to go to Jerusalem and to do what was necessary to promote the rebuilding project. But he knew he'd have to get the king's permission and help first and the king was definitely not a believer. Nehemiah was the king's right hand man and you don't just let a valued guy like that, a guy who would be very difficult to replace, walk away. Nehemiah was asking a leave of absence for three years, to go and rebuild a wall the king had previously ordered not to be rebuilt. So there were significant reasons to ask God for success before he went to talk with the king.

He's not hesitant to pray for success. He's bold in his prayer. Have you ever prayed, "Lord, make me successful!" If you haven't, why haven't you? What is the alternative? Don't make me too bad of a failure? There is nothing wrong with praying for success if what you're doing is for the glory of God. Pray boldly. Pray that God will make you successful in life for the glory of God. That's what Nehemiah did.

The thing is, if I can't ask God to bless what I'm doing, then I'd better start doing something else. If you can't ask God to make you a success at what you're doing, do something else. God doesn't want you to waste your life. William Carey who founded the modern missionary movement used to say, "Expect great things from God; do great things for God." That's a good motto for every Christian.

LOG-ON: MORNING PRAYER

Enter and make these declarations over your life and church (pray each point at least 5 minutes; this is will give you a total of at least 60 minutes in morning prayer).

1. Under the covering of the Superior Blood of Jesus the Christ, Jesus, you are a great deliverer, at the mention of your name, you can command the supernatural to suspend the natural, just like you did for Gideon, in my career, in my business, in my ministry show me a sign of your Almightiness, that will encourage me to take bold step for you in Jesus' name. [Be specific – mention names, places, time, issues etc. etc.].

2. Under the covering of the Superior Blood of Jesus the Christ, I confess that because I believe in the name of Jesus Christ, I am empowered to have dominion over demons, I have authority over every devil, over every sickness and diseases in Jesus' name. [Be specific – mention names, places, time, issues etc. etc.].

3. Under the covering of the Superior Blood of Jesus the Christ, Father I stand on the authority of your word in John 14:14 and I ask in the name of Jesus that every trace of barrenness shall be eradicated in my life this year. I ask in the name of Jesus, that stagnation comes to an end in my career right now, in Jesus' name. I ask in the name of Jesus, that the Lord will hold my right hand and help me to succeed this year in Jesus' name. [Be specific – mention names, places, time, issues, etc. etc.].

4. Under the covering of the Superior Blood of Jesus the Christ, I declare in the Name of Jesus I am a crown of splendor in the Lord's hand, a royal diadem in the hand of my God, in Jesus name. [Be specific – mention names, places, time, issues etc. etc.]

5. Under the covering of the Superior Blood of Jesus the Christ, Jesus you are a strength to the needy, a refuge from storm, a shadow from the heat, and so I declare and decree in the name of Jesus, in every area of my life where I need help, please strengthen me. By your mercy divert every future storm from my career, my business, my ministry and in our nation, in Jesus name. Father in the name of Jesus, insulate me and my family from any stress from the economy, in the name of Jesus. [Be specific – mention names, places, time, issues etc. etc.]

6. Under the covering of the Superior Blood of Jesus the Christ, I declare in the name of Jesus that by the resurrection of the Lord Jesus Christ, I have hope of a better tomorrow. I confess that my situation is not hopeless; my future is secured because Jesus lives. [Be specific – mention names, places, time, issues etc. etc.].

7. Under the covering of the Superior Blood of Jesus the Christ, I confess The Lord Jesus Christ is my Bread of Life. He is the Living Bread that came down from heaven, and because I eat of this Bread, I have life instead of death, in Jesus' name. Because I eat of this Bread, I have peace instead of storm, I have joy instead of sorrow, I have wealth instead of poverty, I have blessings instead of curses, I have honor instead of disgrace, in the name of Jesus.

8. Under the covering of the Superior Blood of Jesus the Christ, I confess in the name of Jesus, that this year and beyond, Jesus Christ will be my compass. I will always fix my eyes on Jesus, the author and the finisher of my faith. I confess that my focus will be on the joy that is waiting for me in the very end. By the help of the Holy Spirit, I will finish strong, in Jesus' name. [Be specific – mention names, places, time, issues etc. etc.].

9. Under the covering of the Superior Blood of Jesus the Christ, I declare the word of the Lord is alive in me, the word gives me strength. I confess the word is sharper than any double-edged sword, cutting between my soul and my spirit, between my joint and my marrow., therefore no sickness can hide in my body, in the name of Jesus. [Be specific – mention names, places, time, issues etc. etc.].

10. Under the covering of the Superior Blood of Jesus the Christ, I declare I cannot be stranded; I will always know what to do on time in all situations, as I receive direction from the Holy Spirit. By the help of the Holy Spirit, my steps shall be ordered by the Lord. I will not make mistakes, in the name of Jesus. I come against every form of spirit of error in my career, in my business and in my ministry, in Jesus' name. [Be specific – mention names, places, time, issues etc. etc.]

11. Under the covering of the Superior Blood of Jesus the Christ, I confess my trust is not in man, but in the promises of God as contained in the word, I rejoice and I am confident that this year will end well for me, therefore I shall not be confused, I shall not be afraid. I declare in the name of Jesus, this

year is a year of testimonies for me. [Be specific –
mention names, places, time, issues etc. etc.]

12. Under the covering of the Superior Blood of Jesus
the Christ, I confess I receive help through the word
to live a holy life. By the help of the Holy Spirit my
life shall conform to the image of our Lord Jesus
Christ. [Be specific – mention names, places, time,
issues etc. etc.]

LOG-OFF: EVENING PRAYER

Enter and make these declarations over your life and
church (pray each point at least 5 minutes; this is will give
you a total of at least 60 minutes in evening prayer).

1. Under the covering of the Superior Blood of Jesus
the Christ, I declare I shall be wise to build my life
on the rock that cannot sink. I confess I will not
build my career, my business, my ministry on
sinking sand, by the help of the Lord. I will only
build upon the rock. I will listen to the words of
Jesus and I will receive grace obey them, in Jesus
name. [Be specific – mention names, places, time,
issues etc. etc.].

2. Under the covering of the Superior Blood of Jesus
the Christ, Father, fill me with the power of the
Holy Ghost. Father fill me to the overflow. Let your
living water flow through me to millions of people
who are thirsty for the truth. Let my life be a

blessing to multitudes. Father, by the power of your spirit put in me solutions that will bring joy to those who are hurting, in Jesus' name. [Be specific – mention names, places, time, issues etc. etc.].

3. Under the covering of the Superior Blood of Jesus the Christ, Father inspire me from your word, to shine brightly with your love and joy to multitudes in different nations of the world. Father help me to stand out as a bright shining light until I see you in glory, in Jesus' name. [Be specific – mention names, places, time, issues etc. etc.].

4. Under the covering of the Superior Blood of Jesus the Christ, I declare I have Salvation and victory through your word. I confess I have access to your shield of victory and your right hand holds me up. This year through your word, you will broaden the path underneath me. My business will be firmly rooted, my career will be unshakable, my ministry will be unstoppable as I receive help from the Lord, in Jesus' name. [Be specific – mention names, places, time, issues etc. etc.].

5. Under the covering of the Superior Blood of Jesus the Christ, Father, please take my hand and lead me on, take my ministry and turn it to a wonder, take my career and make it extra ordinary, take my business and turn it to a blessing, in Jesus' name. [Be specific – mention names, places, time, issues etc. etc.].

6. Under the covering of the Superior Blood of Jesus the Christ, Father, I have no power of my own; please don't abandon me to my enemies. By your mercy I will not be put to shame, I will not be confused; I will receive timely help from the Lord, in

Jesus' name. [Be specific – mention names, places, time, issues etc. etc.].

7.   Under the covering of the Superior Blood of Jesus the Christ, Father, don't let the storm of life sweep me away, by your mercy divert every storm that may blow this year, in Jesus' name. [Be specific – mention names, places, time, issues etc. etc.].

8.   Under the covering of the Superior Blood of Jesus the Christ, Father, please uphold me so that I will never fall and I will never fail, I declare in the name of Jesus, my marriage will not fail, my career will not end suddenly, my business will not be stranded, my ministry will make progress, in the name of Jesus. [Be specific – mention names, places, time, issues etc. etc.].

9.   Under the covering of the Superior Blood of Jesus the Christ, Father, please make me be a channel of blessings; help me so I can help others. Let my life bring multitudes to Jesus. [Be specific – mention names, places, time, issues etc. etc.].

10. Under the covering of the Superior Blood of Jesus the Christ, Father, before this year is over, let me become a living testimony, to the Glory of your Holy Name, by the end of the year, let my testimony be "all is well that ends well". I decree concerning my decisions this year, there shall be no trouble, I declare peace in Jesus name, and God's perfect will for my life shall come to pass, in Jesus' name. I decree in the name of Jesus, every manipulation from men shall be frustrated, in Jesus' name. [Be specific – mention names, places, time, issues etc. etc.].

11. Under the covering of the Superior Blood of Jesus the Christ, In the name of Jesus, this year I will be strong and very courageous, by the help of the Holy Spirit. I will be careful to obey all the Word and voice of God. I confess I will not turn from it to the right or to the left, therefore I will be successful in all my Godly endeavors, in Jesus' name. [Be specific – mention names, places, time, issues etc. etc.].

12. Under the covering of the Superior Blood of Jesus the Christ, Praise the Lord for miracles you have received since the 40-day fast started. Give praise to the Lord for various assistance He has given you. You want to praise him, you want to say "God I thank you for the way you helped me when it looked like I was helpless. Thank you for helping me when no one could help me. Thank you for protecting me when I didn't even know what is called danger. Thank you for helping me when men disappointed me. Father, I am grateful for life. To you be all the Glory, in Jesus' name. [Be specific – mention names, places, time, issues etc. etc.].

DAY 37

It's A Prayer of Adoration

Nehemiah adores who God is. He proclaims that God is a just God, a great God, that God wants to hear prayers and wants to answer prayers. He's acknowledging who God is. Our prayer should always adore God's identity, God's worthiness, God's sovereignty. This is what praise is about. The Prayer of Adoration is not the same as the Prayer of Thanksgiving. Adoration acknowledges God for who He is; whilst Thanksgiving acknowledges God for what He has done. Adoration acknowledges that God is worthy of worship.

The Prayer of Adoration is imperative because it opens God's ears, grants you access into His throne-room, and gives you favor before Him. Adoration is like flattering someone; and when someone is flattered, they show you grace and favor. Nehemiah wanted God to grant Him favor in the sight of the king so he began his prayer with adoration of genuine flattering. When you pray, spend more time, in adoration.

LOG-ON: MORNING PRAYER

Enter and make these declarations over your life and church (pray each point at least 5 minutes; this is will give you a total of at least 60 minutes in morning prayer).

1. Under the covering of the Superior Blood of Jesus the Christ, Lord I praise you from everlasting to everlasting because you are God.
2. Under the covering of the Superior Blood of Jesus the Christ, Father I praise you for your goodness and mercy that has upheld me from January to this day.
3. Under the covering of the Superior Blood of Jesus the Christ, Lord I worship you for who you are; ever merciful and ever true.
4. Under the covering of the Superior Blood of Jesus the Christ, Father I thank you for the miracle of sleeping and waking up.
5. Under the covering of the Superior Blood of Jesus the Christ, Father I magnify you for your amazing grace that has kept me thus far in the journey of life.
6. Under the covering of the Superior Blood of Jesus the Christ, Father I praise you for your goodness and mercy that has upheld me from January to this day.
7. Under the covering of the Superior Blood of Jesus the Christ, Alpha and Omega, I praise you for the grace of waiting upon you in fasting and prayers all these days.

8. Under the covering of the Superior Blood of Jesus the Christ, I am grateful Lord for you are the One working in me to fulfill all your good pleasures.

9. Under the covering of the Superior Blood of Jesus the Christ, Lord I give you praise for your knowledge and wisdom that transcends that of any human being.

10. Under the covering of the Superior Blood of Jesus the Christ, I give you praise because you are a covenant keeping God.

11. Under the covering of the Superior Blood of Jesus the Christ, Father, you are the same yesterday, today and forever. Let me experience your wonderful works again in my life and in my family.

12. Under the covering of the Superior Blood of Jesus the Christ, I praise you O Lord for you are the God that answers prayer.

.

LOG-OFF: EVENING PRAYER

Enter and make these declarations over your life and church (pray each point at least 5 minutes; this is will give you a total of at least 60 minutes in evening prayer).

1. Under the covering of the Superior Blood of Jesus the Christ, Holy Father, I thank You for the blessings I receive every day. I thank You for everything You have done for me. Thank You for

the beauty that surrounds me, thank You for Your provision, for my family and friends, for my health, but most of all, thank You for Your son, Jesus Christ.

2. Under the covering of the Superior Blood of Jesus the Christ, Heavenly Father, thank You for sending Your son Jesus Christ to the cross to take away my sins, my diseases, my pain and my sorrow. Thank You Jesus for Your sacrifice. Thank You that You loved me enough to shed Your blood and die for me, and thank You for my salvation.

3. Under the covering of the Superior Blood of Jesus the Christ, Father, I come to You in the name of the Lord Jesus Christ, entering into Your presence with thanksgiving and a worshipful heart. My soul will bless You for I know the reason behind my creation, and my heart desires to bring You pleasure.

4. Under the covering of the Superior Blood of Jesus the Christ, Praising You for Your mercy and goodness in my past, offering up to You the sacrifice of praise in my present, and thanking You for what You are preparing for my future – this is the joy and purpose of my life.

5. Under the covering of the Superior Blood of Jesus the Christ, You have chosen me in this generation to show forth Your praise, expressing to all how You have called me out of my former darkness into a life filled with light.

6. Under the covering of the Superior Blood of Jesus the Christ, I know when I praise You I am given access to your very Presence. I know that heaven opens up to my life and supernaturally intervenes on my behalf.

7. Under the covering of the Superior Blood of Jesus the Christ, As I magnify You, my troubles are minimized; as I worship Your Name, help is on the way. I choose to praise You. I refuse to permit an unthankful heart to interfere with my inheritance.

8. Under the covering of the Superior Blood of Jesus the Christ, My mind will be filled with thoughts about how good You are. My emotions will release their joy. My body will express itself freely. You alone are God and worthy to be praised, and I will worship none other.

9. Under the covering of the Superior Blood of Jesus the Christ, Praise is going before me and dealing with every evil tactic and scheme of my enemies. Thank You Father, that I am living under an open heaven, free to praise and worship You, the One who loves me with an everlasting love.

10. Under the covering of the Superior Blood of Jesus the Christ, Father, I thank You for every good and perfect gift that You have given to me in Jesus Christ. Thank You for your grace and the gift of salvation by faith. I thank You that Jesus Christ is in me; the Author and Finisher of faith. I have received the faith of God. I will not shrink back in fear, but I will grow in faith and confidence. I will walk by faith and not by sight. I know that faith pleases You. Nothing is impossible for those who choose to believe in You. I place my trust in You. I know that I will never be disappointed or put to shame for doing so. Thank You for the shield You have provided for my defense. Thank You for Your Word that builds my faith in You. I will walk and live by faith under an open heaven of Your possibilities.

11. Under the covering of the Superior Blood of Jesus the Christ, Lord, thank you for sending the Holy Spirit to help me. The Spirit of God is falling into my situation with me; joining me as my Partner, collaborating with me in prayer; becoming a part of my team, and putting me on a right and stable path. I confess that the Holy Spirit is my companion. When I call out to Him in my moments of need, He quickly comes to my rescue. He opens my spiritual eyes and shows me what I cannot see for myself and opens my spiritual ears so that I may hear His voice, and He gives me the right words to say when I pray.

12. Under the covering of the Superior Blood of Jesus the Christ, Lord, thank you that I will stay focused on my calling and remain determined to do what you've called me to do. Your Spirit works mightily in me, giving me all the power I need to resist every assault the enemy tries to bring against me. I boldly confess that I will not stop or give up until I have captured that for which Jesus Christ captured for me. I will successfully achieve all that You have called me to do, for I am determined that I will never stop until I have finished the task. Father, thank you for giving me the stamina and perseverance to get the job done. I can and will do exactly what You, Father, have asked me to do.

DAY 38

It's A Prayer of Admission

Nehemiah admits his inadequacy and the inadequacy of all of God's people. It's acknowledging what I am and who I am; saying "God, I've messed up. I've made mistakes and I'm imperfect." Be specific. The Prayer of Admission is the gateway to deliverance. There's no deliverance without admission. When you check in at the hospital, it is called "admission" because you have admitted to a problem, without which you can't be seen by a doctor. If you want the Great Physician to attend to your problem, then don't hold back on Him. Be very specific and admit everything in detail to Him. The greater the details during the admission, the better the doctor can help you. This is also called the Prayer of Confession. Though the superior blood of Jesus Christ has the potency to deliver from all sins and problems, unconfessed sins, and unconfessed problems, cannot be forgiven and erased by the blood.

Is there something you must admit to and confess thoroughly before Him? This is between you and Him.

LOG-ON: MORNING PRAYER

Enter and make these declarations over your life and church (pray each point at least 5 minutes; this is will give you a total of at least 60 minutes in morning prayer).

1.   Under the covering of the Superior Blood of Jesus the Christ, I confess in the name of Jesus, that I am born of God and the Blood of Jesus Christ makes atonement for my life. I declare that in Him I have redemption through His blood. I confess in the name of Jesus that my sins are wiped away in accordance with the riches of God's grace. I confess that I have been chosen according to the foreknowledge of God the Father, through the sanctifying work of the spirit, for obedience to Jesus Christ and sprinkling by His blood.

2.   Under the covering of the Superior Blood of Jesus the Christ, I declare that the blood of Jesus Christ has cleansed my conscience from acts that lead to death; as a result I am a new man in Christ, serving the living God. I confess I shall experience divine assistance by the blood of Jesus.

3.   Under the covering of the Superior Blood of Jesus the Christ, I confess that the word of the Lord stands forever; I confess that the word of God works for me; I shall receive divine assistance through the word of God. I declare that I am who the word says I am, this year I will receive what the word says I have, in my career, in my business, in my ministry, I will become what the word says I will become. This year I will not speak fear, I will speak the word of faith, that is in me. I will prophesy by faith to every

situation to align with the word of God. I confess I will receive light, instruction and understanding from the word, and by the help of the Holy Spirit, I will be a doer of the Word.

4. Under the covering of the Superior Blood of Jesus the Christ, I declare in the name of Jesus, I am anointed to carry out the dreams and vision given to me by God. I confess that the grace of the Lord abounds on to me and opens me to the gifting deposited in me, my eyes are on the victory despite contrary report. My focus is on my healing and not the sickness, my focus is on my deliverance and not the detrimental situations, my focus is on the miraculous restoration that is on the way and not what I have lost, I declare and decree as I focus on Jesus, my Victory will appear in Jesus name.

5. Under the covering of the Superior Blood of Jesus the Christ, I declare in the name of Jesus, there is now no condemnation for me, because I am in Christ Jesus. I break free from self condemnation, I break free from shame, I break free from self pity, by the help of the Holy Spirit, I eliminate from my life, unprofitable thoughts that have kept me down for too long, I break free from oppression, I break free from confusion, fear and despair. I confess the light of the word of God illuminates my heart, I am victorious, this is my year to harvest Godly great things. Testimonies will meet testimonies in my house, by the power of the Holy Spirit, this year I will swim in super abundance, in Jesus' name.

6. Under the covering of the Superior Blood of Jesus the Christ, I declare in the name of Jesus, that the Lord will open great doors for me this year,

monumental opportunities are coming my way this year. Giant opportunities that will showcase the work of my hands, through the power of the Holy Spirit, will locate me this year. I confess in the name of Jesus, everything I start will finish well this year. God's grace abounds on to me as I carry out His visions for my life. The projects I initiate will be accomplished, in Jesus' name. The Lord, The I AM, will go before me to break every barrier, that may stand before my career or my business, in Jesus' name. This year my business or my career will be a reference point, for promotion, as the Breaker, Jehovah, goes before me. I receive open doors internationally, I enter into a new realm of achievement, in Jesus' name. Father, close every door to devourers in my life. Every anti-testimony, anti-opportunity spirits working against me be paralyzed, in Jesus' name. This year, the work of my hands, my career shall be filled with testimonies; I am victorious, in Jesus' name.

7. Under the covering of the Superior Blood of Jesus the Christ, I declare, and decree in the name of Jesus, my time of waiting is over. This is my season of total victory over sin, over sickness, over barrenness, over debt and over failure, in Jesus' name. I declare that in my life and in my church, a new era of progress, promotion, joy and a closer walk with God has begun. I confess that anxiety and worry will not dominate me. I choose to walk and dwell in the love of God. I am free from condemnation. I declare that in this year, I will be victorious. I am an overcomer though the blood of the Lamb and the word of my testimony, I declare

that every day of this year, I will always overcome the devil and therefore refuse to be moved by what I see. This year I will walk with God by faith and not by sight. I call those things that are not as though they were. I call into existence things by faith, in Jesus' name.

8.   Under the covering of the Superior Blood of Jesus the Christ, I declare in the name of Jesus, that I have been delivered from every form of slavery. I confess that sin does not have dominion over me. I have power over demons. I have been declared righteous through Jesus. I am Holy, and I possess my inheritance in Christ Jesus. I declare my gates of blessings shall be opened continually. They shall not be shut, day nor night, so that men may bring unto me the resources of the gentiles and that their kings may be brought, in Jesus' name

9.   Under the covering of the Superior Blood of Jesus the Christ, I declare in the name of Jesus, that this year, great doors shall be opened to me supernaturally, The Lord shall increase my greatness, and comfort me on every side. I confess I am the righteousness of God, in Christ Jesus. I shall flourish like the palm tree and grow like a cedar in Lebanon, in Jesus' name. I declare that this year, the Lord will open doors that will lead to a good land, a land of brooks, of water, of fountains, and flowing springs; a land with great opportunities, in Jesus' name. I declare in the name of Jesus the door that will be opened to me shall have surplus. There will be no scarcity there, in Jesus' name. I confess as the Lord opens great doors for me, I will recover all my wasted opportunities, in Jesus' name.

10. Under the covering of the Superior Blood of Jesus the Christ, I declare in the name of Jesus, that the Lord will deliver my soul from death and my eyes from weeping. I will not backslide, in the name of Jesus. I confess that the Lord will deliver me out of the mire, I will not sink. I declare that I am delivered from every trouble, by the power of the Spirit, in the name of Jesus. I confess my life shall continually reference the Lord and my days shall be prolonged, in Jesus' name. Father by your mercy, I declare I shall not be taken away in the middle of my days. According to the greatness of your power, you will preserve my life and the life of my loved ones, in the name of Jesus. I cancel every appointment with untimely death, in Jesus' name. I declare I shall live, to declare the goodness of The Lord in the land of the living, in Jesus' name. Every arrow of sudden death, fashioned against me and my family shall not prosper, in Jesus' name. I declare that the Lord shall cover our heads in the days of battle throughout this year, in the mighty name of Jesus

11. Under the covering of the Superior Blood of Jesus the Christ, I confess that Jesus is Lord; He is Lord over my life. I believe that Jesus died for my sins and rose again as proof of my victory. I confess and repent of my sins. Father, by your mercy, wash me clean from all unrighteousness. I reject Satan and all his works today. I hereby confess Jesus as my Lord and savior.

12. Under the covering of the Superior Blood of Jesus the Christ, I declare in the name of Jesus, that I will not backslide. I confess by the help of the Holy.

LOG-OFF: EVENING PRAYER

Enter and make these declarations over your life and church (pray each point at least 5 minutes; this is will give you a total of at least 60 minutes in evening prayer).

1. Under the covering of the Superior Blood of Jesus the Christ, I confess in the name of Jesus, that I have control over my emotions. I will not let any unwholesome talk come out of my month, but only what is helpful for building others up according to their needs and that it may benefit those who listen. In the name of Jesus, I receive grace to be quick to listen, slow to speak, and slow to become angry, in Jesus' name. I declare I shall not be quickly provoked in my spirit, for anger resides in the lap of fools.

2. Under the covering of the Superior Blood of Jesus the Christ, Father, grant me the ability to be slow to anger, grant me grace to overlook injustices, personal affronts and the things that make me upset, in Jesus' name.

3. Under the covering of the Superior Blood of Jesus the Christ, Father, help me not to carry anger in my heart over anything. Father, help me to let go and forgive quickly. Enable me to be patient with all people and situations in Jesus name.

4. Under the covering of the Superior Blood of Jesus the Christ, Father, I want to be like you: slow to anger and abounding in mercy. Father, help me to better understand your mercy toward me, so that I will be able to extend it to others. Help me to be gracious to everyone who comes my way and to be

full of compassion in all situations. Father, keep me from any kind of emotional outbursts or reactions to things that are inspired by my flesh, in Jesus' name.

5. Under the covering of the Superior Blood of Jesus the Christ, Father, help me to always have kind responses to others, even when they are not kind to me. Give me a heart so full of your love that I am not so easily angered by rudeness or insensitivity coming from other people. Father, enable me to live in peace with the people around me, in Jesus' name.

6. Under the covering of the Superior Blood of Jesus the Christ, Father, strengthen me in my inner man, so that I will be able to take control of my emotions. Help me never to have an angry outburst or say things I will later regret. Father, give me a compassionate, loving and patient heart toward others so that I am not even tempted to show anger toward anyone.

7. Under the covering of the Superior Blood of Jesus the Christ, In the name of Jesus, I receive grace to let go and forgive anyone I may have a grudge against, so that my Father in heaven may forgive my sins. In Jesus name, I confess I am kind and compassionate to others, forgiving others just as in Christ, God forgave me. By the help of the Holy Spirit, I will make every effort to live in peace with all men and to be Holy. By the grace of God, I will make it to heaven and I will see the Lord, in Jesus' name.

8. Under the covering of the Superior Blood of Jesus the Christ, Father, by the power of your Spirit, enable me to forgive people as often as it takes. Help

me to always pray for people, instead of judging them.

9. Under the covering of the Superior Blood of Jesus the Christ, Father, search me and see if there is any unforgiveness in me; grant me grace to always confess everything I need to repent of so that I can receive your full forgiveness. Father, by your mercy, let me have the beautiful countenance of someone who is completely right before you.

10. Under the covering of the Superior Blood of Jesus the Christ, Father, help me to forgive all offenders against me – past, present and future. In every situation that I have been judgmental or condemned others, please have mercy and forgive me, in Jesus' name.

11. Under the covering of the Superior Blood of Jesus the Christ, Father, give me the ability to love those who have hurt me, to bless those who have been cruel to me and to be good to those who have behaved badly towards me.

12. Under the covering of the Superior Blood of Jesus the Christ, Father, help me to love others the way you love them. Help me to let go of resentment, or bitterness, in Jesus' name.

DAY 39

It's A Prayer of Assurance

A prayer of assurance is praying the promises of God into manifestation. God's promises can be relied on and we need to live our lives in the light of that truth. God may not answer us based on what we ask, but He is obligated to answer us based on what He has promised. His Word is important to Him. His reputation and integrity depend on His promise (His Word), and He cannot afford to fail to do what He said He'll do. It would make Him a liar. God cannot be a liar. Hence, He is obligated to do what He has promised to do.

The quickest way to have our prayers answered is to stand on the promises of God. It is to take Him hostage on account of His Word. You've got to learn those promises and act in accord with them.

LOG-ON: MORNING PRAYER

Enter and make these declarations over your life and church (pray each point at least 5 minutes; this is will give you a total of at least 60 minutes in morning prayer).

1. Under the covering of the Superior Blood of Jesus the Christ, Father I stand on your word in Matthew 7:7, and I ask that this year, let the heavens be opened over me, let the heavens be opened over the work of my hands. I ask in the name of Jesus that I will have multiple testimonies throughout this year.

2. Under the covering of the Superior Blood of Jesus the Christ, Father, you are the Almighty. This season let your covenant with Abraham be confirmed in my life. I declare that I shall not be barren. I shall be exceedingly fruitful, in the name of Jesus. Genesis 17:1-6.

3. Under the covering of the Superior Blood of Jesus the Christ, I confess my love for Jesus, and as I seek The Lord passionately this year, let riches, honor, enduring wealth and righteousness be my experience this year, in Jesus' name. Proverbs 8:17-18.

4. Under the covering of the Superior Blood of Jesus the Christ, Father in the name of Jesus, I pull down every strange altar I have consciously or unconsciously erected to compete with God in my life, family, business, career or ministry, in Jesus' name. Deuteronomy 32:12, Exodus 20:3, Hosea 4:17.

5. Under the covering of the Superior Blood of Jesus the Christ, Father in the name of Jesus, this year let my faith please you. Inspire me to pursue the things of God diligently, and let me have a proof of your reward in my career, in the work of my hands, in my ministry, in Jesus' name. Hebrews 11:6.

6. Under the covering of the Superior Blood of Jesus the Christ, I declare this year that the Lord's covenant with Abraham is confirmed in me, I am greatly increasing in all areas by His grace. Genesis 17:2.

7. Under the covering of the Superior Blood of Jesus the Christ, I declare in the name of Jesus, that the blessings the Lord will give me shall endure, in Jesus' name. Proverbs 13:22.

8. Under the covering of the Superior Blood of Jesus the Christ, I declare and confess that in this year that I shall be very wealthy in cash and in properties, in the name of Jesus. Genesis 13:2.

9. Under the covering of the Superior Blood of Jesus the Christ, I declare in the name of Jesus, that the work of my hands is blessed this year. Everything I lay my hands upon shall prosper, I will reap a hundred fold return, in Jesus' name. I declare I will be so rich in every sense that I will become the envy of nations. Genesis 26:12, 1.

10. Under the covering of the Superior Blood of Jesus the Christ, I declare in this year, I will be too powerful for my enemies, in the name of Jesus. I declare I cannot be stranded; when one door closes, a better one opens immediately. Genesis 26:16.

11. Under the covering of the Superior Blood of Jesus the Christ, I declare in the name of Jesus in this year, I will blossom through revelation, The Lord inspires me to wealth, I am exceedingly prosperous, I own large estates, flourishing businesses and landmark transactions will pass through my hands, in the name of Jesus. Genesis 30:43.

12. Under the covering of the Superior Blood of Jesus the Christ, I declare I am established firmly in God's purpose for my life, for the Lord my God is with me, and makes me exceedingly great. 2 Chron. 1:1.

LOG-OFF: EVENING PRAYER

Enter and make these declarations over your life and church (pray each point at least 5 minutes; this is will give you a total of at least 60 minutes in evening prayer).

1. Under the covering of the Superior Blood of Jesus the Christ, I take authority over this year in the name of Jesus. I decree that all the creation of God will co-operate with me and that all the elemental forces shall refuse to co-operate with my enemies. I speak to the heavenlies, the earth and the seas, they shall work to my favor this year in the mighty name of Jesus Christ. This is the second, minute, hour, day, week, month and year that the Lord has made and I will rejoice and be glad in it. I decree destruction and frustration upon every power uttering incantations and satanic prayers to capture this year in the mighty name of Jesus. I retrieve this year out of the hands of the evil ones. Spirit of favor, counsel, wealth, wisdom, fear of God, might and power come upon me. I shall excel in every area of my life and nothing shall defile me, I shall possess the gate of my enemies and do the work of God faithfully and without murmuring in the mighty name of Jesus.

2. Under the covering of the Superior Blood of Jesus the Christ, The Lord shall anoint me with the oil of gladness above my fellows. The fire of the enemy shall not burn me. My ears shall hear good news and I shall not hear the voice of the enemy. My

future is secured in Christ, in the name of Jesus. God has created me to do some definite services. He has committed into my hands some assignments which He has not committed to anybody else. He has not created me for no reason. I shall do good. I shall do His work. I shall be an agent of peace. I will trust Him in whatever I do and wherever I am.

3. Under the covering of the Superior Blood of Jesus the Christ, Father, let all your good prophecies concerning my life become realities today, in Jesus' name.

4. Under the covering of the Superior Blood of Jesus the Christ, Father, release upon my life the gift of prophecy; and let whatever I am led by your spirit to prophesy, come to manifestation, in Jesus' name.

5. Under the covering of the Superior Blood of Jesus the Christ, Father, release upon my tongue, the power to decree a thing and for it to be instantly established, in Jesus' name.

6. Under the covering of the Superior Blood of Jesus the Christ, Father, give unto me the grace to pray, until I see the fulfillment of your promises and prophecies over my life, in Jesus' name.

7. Under the covering of the Superior Blood of Jesus the Christ, Father, help me to use the gift of prophecy in my life, to turn the hearts of men to believe in you and to serve you, and not for personal gain, in Jesus' name.

8. Under the covering of the Superior Blood of Jesus the Christ, Father, let all your outstanding

prophecies and overdue promises for my life and family, come into full manifestation, today, in Jesus' name.

9. Under the covering of the Superior Blood of Jesus the Christ, Father, thank you for the gift of prophecy given to me. I believe I am anointed in Jesus name.

10. Under the covering of the Superior Blood of Jesus the Christ, Father, thank you for your unfailing promises over my life and destiny.

11. Under the covering of the Superior Blood of Jesus the Christ, Father, in any way in which I have fallen short of your glory, please, have mercy and forgive me, in Jesus' name.

12. Under the covering of the Superior Blood of Jesus the Christ, Father, I believe and declare you are a covenant keeping God. You keep Your Word. You do not lie. What You say is what You shall do. Hence, I stand upon Your word and promises, and I claim them. I claim your word that Your thoughts toward me are love and peace and I believe you will give me an expected end, a great future, and a glorious breakthrough this year, in Jesus' name.

DAY 40

It's A Prayer of Action

Nehemiah was willing to be part of the answer; to do what needed to be done. We must be ready to say, "I'm willing to be part of the answer. God, You can use me. I commit myself. I'll be part of the solution." Sometimes the answers to our prayers may take longer because God has no available vessel to use. Those who have worked with God in the past have learned the secret of making themselves an answer to their prayer. When Isaiah had prayed, God asked Him, "who shall I send?". And Isaiah responded sharply, "here am I LORD, send me." Had he not given that answer, the answer to his prayer could've taken longer, until God finds a willing vessel in you. Sometimes, you're the answer to your prayer request. Nehemiah had to give up everything; his job as cupbearer and the most faithful confidant of the king. What will you give up in order to act on your prayer? Is God telling you to surrender to what He wants to do? Sometimes you're praying something will happen for your family to be saved, and God is saying I need someone I can use to speak to them. Are you going to be that person? Sometimes, you're praying that God will change your friends, or the young people and bring a change in our society, and God is saying, "yes you got that right, but I need someone I can use for this." Will you take action and sign up? Moses asked God at the burning bush encounter, "have you heard the cry of Your people in Egypt?" God responded, "Go, and tell Pharaoh, let My people go." Is God speaking to you to be His vessel for this prayer request?

Finally, Nehemiah understood what every believer must know, - that believers influence their world. If they don't then they're probably not believers. Jesus made it clear at His ascension that we're the light of this world, and the salt of the earth. Each of us influences the world in some way. We either influence it for God, influence it to get our own selfish desires, influence it negatively, or allow it to be influenced by the broken, impersonal forces of this world. The issue isn't whether you're influencing the world or not, it's whether you're a good influencer or not. The first step to being a good, Godly influencer is to develop a passionate prayer life; time alone with God as part of a personal, daily, devoted relationship. Learn to pray like Nehemiah prayed and watch what God will do.

LOG-ON: MORNING PRAYER

Enter and make these declarations over your life and church (pray each point at least 5 minutes; this is will give you a total of at least 60 minutes in morning prayer).

1. Under the covering of the Superior Blood of Jesus the Christ, This year, I put myself and members of my family into the protective envelope of divine fire, in the name of Jesus.
2. Under the covering of the Superior Blood of Jesus the Christ, This year, I will do the will of God and I will serve God, in the name of Jesus.
3. Under the covering of the Superior Blood of Jesus the Christ, This year, I will have unconquerable victory, in Jesus' name.
4. Under the covering of the Superior Blood of Jesus the Christ, This year, like a clay in the hands of the potter, the Lord will make what He wants out of my life, in the name of Jesus.
5. Under the covering of the Superior Blood of Jesus the Christ, This year, the Lord will do with me whatever He wants, in the name of Jesus.
6. Under the covering of the Superior Blood of Jesus the Christ, This year, the Lord will make me the head and not the tail, in Jesus' name.
7. Under the covering of the Superior Blood of Jesus the Christ, This year, every snare of the fowler assigned against me shall perish, in Jesus' name.
8. Under the covering of the Superior Blood of Jesus the Christ, This year, I render the habitation of darkness assigned against me desolate, in the name of Jesus.

9. Under the covering of the Superior Blood of Jesus the Christ, This year, divine deposits shall settle in my life, in the name of Jesus.

10. Under the covering of the Superior Blood of Jesus the Christ, This year, I enter into the covenant of favor, in the name of Jesus.

11. Under the covering of the Superior Blood of Jesus the Christ, This year, the anointing of success and fruitfulness shall rest on me, in the name of Jesus.

12. Under the covering of the Superior Blood of Jesus the Christ, This year, I will not be a candidate of laboring without result, in Jesus' name.

LOG-OFF: EVENING PRAYER

Enter and make these declarations over your life and church (pray each point at least 5 minutes; this is will give you a total of at least 60 minutes in evening prayer).

1. Under the covering of the Superior Blood of Jesus the Christ, This year, all obstacles in my way of progress shall be dismantled, in the name of Jesus.

2. Under the covering of the Superior Blood of Jesus the Christ, This year, my God shall arise and my stubborn pursuers shall scatter, in Jesus' name.

3. Under the covering of the Superior Blood of Jesus the Christ, This year, those that mock me in the past

shall celebrate with me, in Jesus' name.

4. Under the covering of the Superior Blood of Jesus the Christ, This year, I shall be unstoppable against all forces of darkness, in the name of Jesus.

5. Under the covering of the Superior Blood of Jesus the Christ, This year, every power assigned to cut short my life shall die, in the name of Jesus.

6. Under the covering of the Superior Blood of Jesus the Christ, This year, my prayers shall always provoke angelic violence for my good, in Jesus' name.

7. Under the covering of the Superior Blood of Jesus the Christ, This year, I shall speak and my words shall bring testimonies, in the name of Jesus.

8. Under the covering of the Superior Blood of Jesus the Christ, Father, let me enjoy the full benefits of your Name this year.

9. Under the covering of the Superior Blood of Jesus the Christ, Father, where there is no way make a way for me this year.

10. Under the covering of the Superior Blood of Jesus the Christ, Father, let me experience your presence and guidance in everything I do this year.

11. Under the covering of the Superior Blood of Jesus the Christ, Father, give me your full backing, support and assistance this year.

12. Under the covering of the Superior Blood of Jesus the Christ, Father, keep the heavens open wide over me this year.

8

The Last Day

Congratulations! You made it! You are on the very last day! Did you ever think it would go by so quickly?!

I'm proud of you for persevering to the end. I've received a few messages from fasters who struggled and contemplated throwing in the towel. But God reminded them this is a marathon, not a sprint; if you fall, you can get back up and run to the finish line. Now...here you are! A few hours away from the finish line! Let's finish well!

How to End Your Fast Physically

If you've been on a full fast for forty days, be careful how you reintroduce food to your system. Most people who are otherwise healthy should be able to return to normal eating within one week of a forty day fast.

There is a period of adjustment, though. This is because two things have happened to the digestive system during a prolonged fast:

1. The stomach has been slowly shrinking. By the end of the fast, the stomach's capacity for food is nothing like it was at the beginning. Even the smallest amount of food can make you feel full.
2. The organs in the body that are usually involved with assimilating food have taken a rest. You could think of it as if the organs have gone into a kind of sleep which became deeper as the fast was extended.

Therefore, when you break your fast, be careful regarding:

1. How much you eat,
2. What you eat,
3. How you eat it.

Give your stomach time to return to its normal size and the digestive organs time to "wake up" fully.

When breaking a fast, some foods are more suitable than others. A fast of great length is best broken with fruit or vegetable juices, if possible, freshly squeezed or juiced. Some consider citrus fruits to be the best. However, if you live where citrus fruits are imported, this is not the best option as they're often picked unripe and the juice can be too acidic. Watermelon juice is excellent, as is tomato, grape or apple juice.

Start with a small quantity, diluted if necessary. Drink it every two to three hours the first day. Increase the quantity gradually and you'll soon be able to take the fruit itself. At this point, milk can be taken. Milk in the form of yogurt taken with fruit would be beneficial.

Gradually return to regular eating with several small snacks during the first few days. Start with a little soup and fresh fruit such as watermelon and cantaloupe. Advance to a few tablespoons of solid foods such as raw fruits and vegetables or a raw salad and baked potato.

Fresh salad (no dressing), vegetable soups (no fat), and cooked vegetables may be included at this point, always starting with a small amount of anything new and gradually increasing.

Next, you could include a little toasted bread with a small slice of butter, but no cakes, pastries or cookies. Starchy foods are not good at this stage. Introduce protein first in the form of cheese or eggs (or Greek yogurt), with fish and meat last of all.

Eat slowly; chew thoroughly. Chew your food well so that it is reduced to liquid before swallowing. When you begin to feel full, stop eating.

Rest as much as you can during the period of reintroducing

food to your system. It will let your body concentrate on digestion and assimilation. Try not to become too active too soon.

How to End Your Fast Spiritually

Although you can relax physically, do not relax spiritually! You can't afford to. Your enemy, the devil, prowls like a roaring lion seeking someone to devour (1 Peter 5:8-9). You must remain alert and vigilant. The "thief" will be on the prowl to steal the increased intimacy with Christ you've gained during your fast.

No doubt, as you've fasted and subjected your flesh to the Spirit, your spiritual ears have become more alert to the voice of the Holy Spirit. Consequently, you're now far more sensitive to even the smallest disobedience and sin in your life...maybe even things you used to do daily that grieved Him and quenched His presence. Satan will now try to get you to cater to your flesh once again. He'll try to clog your spiritual hearing and get you back into areas of disobedience and unyieldedness. Oh, it will be subtle all right. It won't even seem like it's happening. After all, eating returns to normal...why not everything else? Be careful! Be alert! Be intentional! Be disciplined, fellow soldier. Stay disciplined in your prayer time and pursuit of God. Stay disciplined in your submission and quick obedience to the Lord.

How Do You Plan to Keep Fasting a Part of Your Lifestyle?

I'm so glad that you joined ifast 40 Days of Spiritual Development and engaged in the life-changing power of fasting! Please note, though, that a single fast is not a spiritual cure-all. Just as we need fresh infillings of the Holy Spirit daily, we also need fresh times of fasting. Consider a 24-hour fast each week or fasting the first day of the month. I encourage you to pray about it today and make a commitment as to how you plan to keep fasting a part of your lifestyle. It will be hard to make this decision once you get back into old routines of eating. Pray about it now, while the spiritual benefits of fasting are fresh on your mind and in your spirit. When God leads you as to what your regular fasting commitment should be, put it on your calendar — just as you would schedule a meeting for work, a special anniversary, or ladies, your hair appointment. When it's on your calendar, it's a commitment to be kept, not a contingency that can be cancelled.

If You Feel You Failed

It takes time to build your fasting muscles. If you failed to make it through this first fast, do not be discouraged! You may have simply gotten over-zealous and bitten off more than you could chew in terms of choosing too extreme of a fast for your first time. (Try beginning with a simple fasting schedule, breaking early and working around your work schedule. Then on your next fast, go on a full fast for one day. Then possibly fast for three days on your fast after that. God will lead you and enable you to succeed. Don't give up!) Or you may need to strengthen your resolve. As soon as possible, undertake another fast until you do succeed. Even if it is just for one day — or one week. God will honor you for your faithfulness.

Your Testimony

Are you glad that you fasted? If so, why? What positive benefits have you already experienced? I would love for you to share your experience. (Feel free to write me by email or visit my social media page with your comments and testimony). I realize that not all effects of a fast will be immediate. Many benefits will be experienced all year long this year, next year, and the years to come. However, if your fasts are anything like mine, something in the spirit has already changed as a result of your fast. Something in the natural man broke. And for some people, God has already given answers to prayer!

Your fasting testimony will encourage me, but more importantly, it will give glory to God and encourage others in their own seasons of fasting and prayer.